MANAGERIAL LITERACY

WHAT TODAY'S MANAGERS MUST KNOW TO SUCCEED

Gary Shaw
Jack Weber

Dow Jones-Irwin
Homewood, Illinois 60430

Sponsoring editor: Jim Childs
Project editor: Jane Lightell
Production manager: Bette K. Ittersagen
Jacket design: Renee Klyczek Nordstrom
Compositor: Carlisle Communications, Ltd.
Typeface: 11/13 Century Schoolbook
Printer: R. R. Donnelley & Sons Company

Library of Congress Cataloging-in-Publication Data

Shaw, Gary
    Managerial literacy : what today's managers must know to succeed
by Gary Shaw and Jack Weber.
        p.   cm.
    Includes bibliographical references.
    ISBN 1-55623-262-4
    1. Management—Terminology.   2. Executives—Language.
3. Executive ability.   I. Weber, Jack   II. Title.
HD30.15.S48   1990
658.4'0014—dc20   89–17211
                                                                   CIP

Printed in the United States of America
1 2 3 4 5 6 7 8 9 0 DO 6 5 4 3 2 1 0 9

To the managers who helped us to crystallize

the idea of managerial literacy and to shape the list.

This book belongs to them.

CONTENTS

Preface   vii
Acknowledgments   xiii

1   THE LANGUAGE OF BUSINESS   1

     Managerial Literacy in a Changing Business Environment   3
     Language and Literacy   9
     Managerial Literacy and Cultural Literacy   13
     The Managerial Literacy List   17
     The Limits of Literacy   20
     Beyond Literacy   23

2   CRAFTING THE MANAGERIAL LITERACY LIST   26

     Crafting the Right List   26
     Words, Words, Words   27
     Discovering the Limits of the List   29
     Generating the List   30
     Drawing in the Boundaries: Editing and Testing the List   31
     Characteristics of the Managerial Literacy List   42
     The Threshold of Literacy   47

3   IMPLICATIONS FOR MANAGERS   50

     Understanding One's Literacy: Implications and
          Importance of the List   52
     Improving One's Literacy: The Dynamics of Experience
          and Education in Management Development   55
     Enhancing Others' Literacy: Organizational
          Responsibility   64
     Literacy and Leadership   72

4   THE MANAGERIAL LITERACY LIST   75

     The Managerial Literacy List: A Checklist   77

Appendix   THE MANAGERIAL LITERACY LIST: ALPHABETIZED
           VERSION   123

PREFACE

This book establishes the elements and boundaries of managerial literacy by isolating the core knowledge required by managers to succeed in today's fast-changing business environment. We have written the book primarily for managers and executives in American enterprise who are curious about how what they know—and what they don't know—enables or constrains them in dealing with the business opportunities of the 1990s. Through extensive interviews and surveys, we have compiled a list of the critical concepts, words, and phrases that experienced managers draw upon in their everyday conversations and see as central to their own and other managers' success. The managerial literacy list brings into sharp focus for the first time the essential elements of knowledge that shape the way effective managers think, speak, listen, and act.

The idea of managerial literacy compels a new approach to the language of business and offers managers fresh insights into managerial effectiveness. For thoughtful and ambitious middle managers, *Managerial Literacy* provides both the impetus and the means to take charge of their own professional development. This initiative is particularly important in a decade sure to be marked by new competition, continued mergers and acquisitions, and unforeseen global alliances, a period in which career dislocations and opportunities will present themselves unexpectedly. For human resource professionals, line managers, and others entrusted with training, management development, and career planning, the book suggests innovative ways of thinking about the education of managers. Our book also aims to provide senior executives with a new perspective on the scope and sufficiency of managerial knowledge in their organizations, thereby revealing the sources of communication breakdowns and the often-hidden potential for organizational change. For non-American representatives of foreign multinationals, the book provides access to the language of American business. Finally, for our academic colleagues, we hope this book will spur healthy debate and research on the nature and role of managerial literacy in the lifelong learning of American managers.

Readers who have time for books outside the field of management may correctly guess that our book was inspired in part by the best-seller, *Cultural Literacy: What Every American Needs to Know.* Written by Professor E. D. Hirsch, Jr., a colleague in the English Department at the University of Virginia, the book boldly challenges the educational tradition of Rousseau, John Dewey, and others who have disparaged "the piling up of information."[1] Hirsch argues that some information is worth piling up. Asserting that "to be culturally literate is to possess the basic information needed to thrive in the modern world,"[2] he has ignited a national controversy by publishing a list of words and phrases "intended to illustrate the character and range of the knowledge literate Americans tend to share."[3]

Anticipating our own work and interests, Hirsch noted that "the fact that middle-level executives no longer share literate background knowledge is the chief cause of their inability to communicate."[4] We argue that the chief cause of poor communication in business is not the erosion of this broad-based *cultural* knowledge, although this ignorance does contribute to the problem. The chief cause is that managers may not share enough background knowledge within their own professional precincts. Failing to register allusions to Greta Garbo, Handel, or the Alamo (all on Hirsch's list), although regrettable, is less

---

[1]John Dewey and Evelyn Dewey, *Schools of Tomorrow* (New York: Dutton, 1915 [14th printing, 1924]), p. 13.

[2]E. D. Hirsch, Jr., *Cultural Literacy: What Every American Needs to Know* (Boston: Houghton Mifflin, 1987), p. xiii.

[3]Hirsch, *Cultural Literacy,* p. 146.

[4]Hirsch, *Cultural Literacy,* pp. 9–10.

compromising for a manager than not registering references to strategic planning, Fortress Europe, profit center, joint venture, marketing mix, operating income, or economies of scale. Hirsch wants to tell us how to be educated citizens. We, on the other hand, are trying to show what managers and executives ought to know within their profession to remain educated in the idioms, terms, and concepts at the heart of their daily transactions and conversations.

Hirsch's book accelerated our growing interest in the uncharted connection between management and literacy and the implications of this connection for management education. But we realized that the ideas and aims in his discussions of literacy are not perfectly consonant with our own. As a result, we narrowed our focus to the particular language community of American business and determined what subset of information is peculiar to that community. *Managerial literacy* refers to that subset, and this book is the first step in our commitment to isolating the basic knowledge that literate managers and executives regularly draw upon in the course of their work.

In Chapter 1, The Language of Business, we suggest that business managers rely more on language in accomplishing their day-to-day goals than they often acknowledge. Building on the work of Hirsch and on some fundamental business literature, we argue that management depends preeminently on the art of conversation, and we claim that the shared vocabulary drawn upon by managers and executives is the basis of sound communication, managerial effectiveness, and a coherent corporate culture. Managerial literacy thus represents the present benchmark for what is said and done in contemporary business and gives managers access to a set of connections and evocations that can extend their present knowledge and influence.

In Chapter 2, Crafting the Managerial Literacy List, we lay out the methods and guidelines we used to map the boundaries of the language community of American business. Our approach involved examining business periodicals and classic texts in both general management and the core functions of business (e.g., marketing, accounting, finance, operations, human resource management). We had conversations with business school professors in the various disciplines and conducted interviews with hundreds of practicing managers and executives, from middle managers to CEOs. Finally, we administered a national, multi-industry survey of executives and managers at some of the most respected and successful corporations in America. This research allowed us to reduce a preliminary list of nearly 2,500 items to the present list of 1,200 terms. Our close work with the list and our attention to the key issues in crafting it led us to comment on its overall shape and characteristics.

In Chapter 3, Implications for Managers, we explore those implications of managerial literacy that extend beyond the particular aspects of the list. We outline several ways that managers can use the list to spur their own and other managers' professional development. We came to see that literacy develops differently in different managers. Interviews and conversations with a broad cross section of experienced managers and executives (who had not been involved with the actual development of the list) provoked us to speculate further about the changing needs of American business managers and the role of education, both formal and informal, in responding to these needs. Finally, we suggest the importance to business leaders of providing an environment and culture that nourishes managerial literacy and lifelong learning.

In Chapter 4, we present the refined and tested list of business-related words, phrases, abbreviations, and concepts in the form of a checklist. Many of these items—*Theory X, junk bond, type A, shark repellent, LBO, Black Monday, the 80–20 rule, tombstone*—occur regularly without explanation or definition because literate American managers are expected to be implicitly familiar with these words and their underlying associations. The final list thus contains the basic information shared by successful top executives and middle managers in American corporations. As such, it represents the language of current managerial practice and can be used to gauge individual literacy levels and to detect changes in the larger business environment. For educators and directors of executive development programs and "corporate universities," the list will provide an instrument for evaluating curricula and for aligning academic programs with American business practice. Individual managers can of course use the list informally to test and educate themselves. A quick review of the managerial literacy checklist will highlight the most important concepts, expressions, and idioms used in the offices, around the conference tables, and within the boardrooms of corporate America. We hope, moreover, that the managerial literacy list will open up new avenues of research into the important role of literacy in lifelong learning and managerial effectiveness.

Gary Shaw
Jack Weber

ACKNOWLEDGMENTS

The success of a project of this scope depends upon the many people who support the authors. We are therefore deeply grateful to acknowledge the many debts we've incurred in developing and writing this book. First, we'd like to thank the hundreds of practicing managers and executives from the following companies and organizations who freely offered their time and insight in developing the list:

American Cyanamid
American Trucking Associations, Inc.
Arnold & Porter
Arthur Andersen & Company
AT&T
AT&T Canada, Inc.
AT&T Technologies
Automotive Replacement Glass
Banker's Trust Company
Bell Atlantic
The BF Goodrich Company
Blue Cross & Blue Shield of Virginia
Boeing Corporation
Boston Properties
British Petroleum
Wm. Byrd Press, Inc.
C&P Telephone Company of Virginia
The Capital Hilton
Cadmus Communications Corporation
Catawba Timber Company

Chesapeake Corporation
Chesapeake National Bank
Chesebrough-Pond's, Inc.
Citicorp
Coca-Cola Company
Colonial Williamsburg Hotel Properties, Inc.
Commonplace Price Company
Connecticut National Bank
Court & Donovan
Cresap, McCormick & Paget
Department of Defense
Department of the Navy
Digital Equipment Corporation
Eastman Chemical Products, Inc.
Edgewood Management Company
Elida Gibbs Ltd.
ERC International
Exxon Corporation
Figgie Leasing Corporation
Florida Power & Light Company
Frito Lay Inc.
General Electric Company
General Tire
George J. Meyer Manufacturing
Gilbert Commonwealth, Inc.
The Gillette Company
GM (Pontiac Division)
Harbridge House
Hartford Life Insurance Company
Hickory Business Furniture
IBM Corporation
James River Corporation
Kaempfer Company
Kemper Corporation
Landmark Communications, Inc.
Lever Brothers Company
The Life Insurance Company of Virginia
Lindsay Saker Limited
MacMillan Bloedel Inc.

Macy's
Marriott Corporation
Martin Marietta Energy Systems
Massachusetts Financial Services Co.
McKinsey & Company
Merrill Lynch & Co., Inc.
Messalin Particulares
Monitor Company
National Starch & Chemical Co., Inc.
NYNEX Corporation
Ohio Power Company
Omni Construction, Inc.
Pacific Bell
Palmer & Dodge
Paper Manufacturers Company Inc.
Peterbilt Motors Company
Philip Morris Companies, Inc.
Pizza Hut, Inc.
Price Waterhouse
Procter & Gamble Co.
Public Service Corporation of Oklahoma
Ralston Purina Corporation
Reynolds Metals Company
Royal Bank of Canada
Ryland Acceptance Corporation
Salomon Brothers Inc.
Security Pacific Bank
Shearson Lehman Brothers Inc.
Shedd's Food Products, Inc.
Southern Bell Co.
Southland Waste Systems
Sovran Bank, Inc.
Spaulding & Slye
Springs Industries, Inc.
Stew Leonard's
Syntex Laboratories
T. Rowe Price
Texaco Chemical Company
Thomas J. Lipton, Inc.

Touche Ross & Company
The Travelers Company
Unichema International Division
Unilever United States, Inc.
Warner-Lambert Company
Westpac Banking Corporation

We owe a special debt of gratitude to friends and colleagues who made unique contributions to our work. Tony Baglioni plowed through reams of data with us to help make sense of them. Libby Eshbach provided valuable research support. Bette Collins read draft after draft of chapters and made hundreds of helpful editorial recommendations. Professors Thomas C. MacAvoy, John L. Colley, and Louis Rader (emeritus) reviewed the final list and commented thoughtfully on its design and implications. Our editor, Jim Childs, shepherded us carefully over the arduous terrain of putting together and publishing a book. Our wives, Kate and Carol, and our families supported us in ways nobody else could—or would. And our colleagues at the School of Business at the College of William and Mary and the Darden Graduate School of Business of the University of Virginia gave us both financial and moral support. Their encouragement of the project has done more than we can say.

Finally, a special acknowledgment is due to one person whose help was indispensable. We want to thank our friend, James P. Soderholm, for his tireless work and outstanding contribution to every aspect of this project. His skill, wit, flexibility, sense of purpose, and understanding made him invaluable. We were lucky to work with him.

CHAPTER 1

THE LANGUAGE OF BUSINESS

How to apply for a job,
How to advance from the mailroom,
How to sit down at a desk,
How to dictate memoranda,
How to develop executive style,
How to commute, in a three-button suit,
    with that weary executive smile.
How to observe personnel,
How to select whom to lunch with,
How to avoid petty friends,
How to begin making contacts,
How to enter a conference room with an idea, a brilliant idea,
    that will make your expense account zoom.
This book is all that I need,
How to, how to succeed!

—F. Loesser *How to Succeed in Business (without Really Trying)*

On October 14, 1961, a musical opened on Broadway in which the hero, J. Pierrepont Finch, a young man just entering the corporate ranks, buys a book that purports to tell him how to succeed in business. The book offers him practical instruction about keeping one's footing on the way up the corporate ladder. By following the book's step-by-step advice, the hero does indeed rise quickly and gloriously through the ranks. But the book gives the ambitious J. Pierrepont the dubious wisdom consistent with a view of business prevalent only in satire and musical comedy. From that skewed perspective, the business world appears composed of shallow and uninteresting people with meager talents who perform largely meaningless tasks of exaggerated importance. This view could hardly be further from the truth.

Frank Loesser's musical, *How to Succeed in Business (without Really Trying),* was not the first parody of the get-ahead attitude in American business, but it did focus attention for the first time on another popular American craze also concerned with the prerequisites for success, the "how-to" book. The how-to thrives on the idea that neither experience nor theory, but practical step-by-step instruction, is the only way to gain knowledge or expertise, never mind the complexity of the task or the nature of the endeavor. Most how-tos, like Loesser's, trivialize the ends of any given endeavor—success in business, for example—by making the means to those ends trivial or by suggesting that there is only one way to accomplish them. *How to Succeed* was a good parody in part because it substituted a trivialized set of skills, talents, and knowledge for true business know-how.

A large part of the humor of Loesser's comic tribute to business consists in recognizing how naive, cynical, and artless one must be to believe in the virtues of the how-to and other magic formulas for success. The persistence, however, of less obviously comic how-tos and other quick-fix, self-help books suggests that some people still believe that success in business takes little more than a positive attitude and a few social skills. In contrast, this book takes success in business seriously. It stresses the ongoing need for education because the authors believe there is an important core of knowledge that underlies management effectiveness and that has a lot to do with how managers function in their jobs, in their organizations, and in the larger business community. With the help of managers and executives across the country, the authors were able to isolate the basic elements of managerial expertise needed to build sound businesses and successful careers.

This book is concerned with that kind of expertise, with what it really takes to succeed in business. It is also intended to be very practical, but it offers no magic formula or new management wondertheory. This book is not another how-to. Instead, it focuses on what kind of knowledge success requires and explains why some kinds of knowledge are more important than other kinds. In short, this book defines the range of basic information that practicing managers need to know to function effectively in an increasingly complex and fast-changing business world. These efforts get us back to basics at a time when it is easy to get lost in the outer reaches of both theory and practice. For that reason, this work defines a kind of basic literacy—*managerial literacy*. This first chapter describes the contours and dimensions of this new form of literacy.

MANAGERIAL LITERACY IN A CHANGING BUSINESS ENVIRONMENT

Few managers have cause to doubt that the American business scene is undergoing vast changes. A glance at the business press is enough to provide a sense of the global challenges, the national issues, and the local influences exerting strong pressures to change the way we think about doing business. Consider these few examples:

- The wave of mergers and acquisitions, downsizings, and divestitures has littered the corporate world with dislocated careers and eroded confidence in the social value of such financial restructuring.
- Deregulation of fundamental industries, such as banking and telecommunications, has created exciting new business opportunities at the same time as it has forced massive reorganizations and opened the doors to new competition.
- Individual, corporate, and industrywide performance is currently under greater scrutiny by shareholders and other stakeholders as ethical and financial dealings get more and more media attention.
- Broad demographic shifts in America's "melting pot" are creating a new diversity in the work force and in the marketplace.
- The unprecedented development of computer resources and the application of information technologies in the workplace have brought about possibilities, efficiencies, and problems unimaginable a decade ago.

- The success of the Japanese and other Pacific Rim countries in entering world markets has made us look hard at our productivity, quality, and management style.
- The prospects of a unified European Community and free trade with Canada are forcing American business to reexamine its deep-seated provincialism and to explore international markets and global alliances.

These examples of the profound changes taking place all around us underscore the pervasive problems and challenges facing management today. Smart managers worry about what kind of knowledge can prepare them to work in this environment and handle the myriad problems that will surely crop up. Experience in business—the practical knowledge gained from facing and solving problems—has always counted for a lot. The single greatest problem, therefore, posed by changes in the business environment is that the changes reduce the applicability and clarity of the lessons gained from experience and hindsight. The increasing speed and magnitude of these changes make it hard for managers to be confident about the value of their experience and expertise. It is getting harder for managers to be sure about how well prepared they are to deal with emerging managerial perspectives, changing tasks, and new roles.

Managerial Literacy in the Business Community

The explosion of knowledge and information has confounded conventional notions of managerial assets and liabilities. The drive to specialize, which has taken hold of business as much or more than it has the sciences, may represent a terrible loss of potential. In traditional businesses organized along functional lines, marketing expertise often remains largely in the marketing area, financial expertise in the finance area. A great danger of this sort of overspecialization is the fragmentation of knowledge that goes with it. The development of narrow technical expertise, if unsupported by a broad knowledge of what else is going on in business, leads directly to the kinds of failure and missed opportunities with which American business has become all too familiar. Very recently, for example, computer experts and information-technology specialists have risen in status, but their specialized training and isolation often render them incapable of making the kind of practical contribution that business wants and needs.

Specialization not only adds to the burden of increased knowledge; it adds to the difficulty—and increases the necessity—of sharing useful information across functional lines and up and down organizational hierarchies. The experience of science serves as a warning lesson here. Working in closely related but increasingly narrow and fragmented fields, scientists have found out, often belatedly, that they cannot talk to one another or use each other's expertise to solve mutual problems.[1] In business, the dangers of this sort of fragmentation are even more critical than in science, because the practical application of most business activity is more immediate and palpable than that of scientific inquiry. This story highlights the problem:

> A young manager, recently promoted to project leader in the systems development area of a large consumer products firm, was charged with developing a comprehensive billing system for internal use. Because he had no real familiarity, however, with the accounting and operations terms needed to understand the requirements of the system's users, he got a distorted sense of their needs when he talked with them. He and the five programmers in his area spent six months developing the specifications, but, upon review, the system was rejected. It showed so little understanding of the common business transactions in billing that it was virtually worthless. The cost to the corporation and to the managers involved was enormous.

Business can ill afford the losses that result from this kind of scenario in the corporate world—losses in time, flexibility, and purpose, as well as in dollars.

---

[1]Alvin Weinberg, the head of Oak Ridge Laboratory, in his book, *Reflections on Big Science* (Cambridge: M. I. T. Press, 1967), p. 44, tells several stories about the irreconcilable differences among practitioners in closely related fields. One such story shows clearly how out of hand the problems of fragmentation can get:

Hydrologists had for many years used an equation to describe the flow of incompressible fluids that left out an important term; hydrodynamicists . . . knew the right equation, but because hydrologists did not speak much with hydrodynamicists, this point in theoretical hydrology contradicted laws of hydrodynamics, and no one was very alarmed about the situation.

Moreover, when managers do cross functional lines, and when they are promoted into positions of greater responsibility or become general managers, their ability to speak a common language becomes more important than any technical expertise per se. The best way, therefore, to ensure that managers become aware of the potential for failure in these situations is to offer these managers a benchmark for what is being currently thought and said throughout the domains of American business. Managers can then identify and fill in the gaps in their knowledge.

As business becomes more complex, more global, and more complicated by social and political pressures, and as the pressures to specialize mount, to isolate the critical elements of managerial knowledge becomes even more important. Many managers do recognize that their ability to work together with other people, to communicate with and to get things done through other people, represents a skill so fundamental to business that we easily forget that it, too, needs developing. But there is no technical expertise or specialization that corresponds to this skill. Developing this ability means setting aside the demands of specialization and focusing on the broad forms of knowledge that allow managers to cope with a wide range of problems, from the specific to the general, from the singular to the persistent. Effectiveness in the business world means recognizing a community of interests and people whose diverse energies, intuitions, and talents may be applied to the range of problems managers have to face.

Peter Kann, the publisher of *The Wall Street Journal,* in an open letter to readers, noted that the business community achieved a national identity over 30 years ago. Reflecting on the decisions and changes that allowed the *Journal* to keep up with its readership despite the accelerating rate of change in business and in society in general, Kann pointed to an important shift in the concept of the business community in the period between 1940 and 1960. The *Journal*'s editors and publishers redefined its market because, he said, "A national business community was perceived, in which the business person in Portland, Maine, had the same information needs as the business person in

Portland, Oregon."[2] This community now extends far beyond our national boundaries. But this basic recognition provides confirmation of an important concept underlying the efforts behind this book: only in a relatively coherent community is there likely to be widespread agreement about what's useful, what needs to be talked about, and what should go without saying.[3] The diversity of enterprises, activities, and people within the broad business community constitutes one of its great strengths, even though such diversity often obscures the shared, or sharable, interests and expertise imbedded in this community. The shared knowledge that has survived the many changes in the business environment shows up in the language managers use daily. This common language is partly what binds the business community together *as a community.*

Kann's point about the business community gains additional support from our national efforts at management education and training. The impressive growth in undergraduate and graduate business programs around the country in the last 30 years is partly a response to the developing sense of a broad business discipline. It's easy to forget now, in this age of the professionally trained manager, that business was not always considered a discipline of sufficient academic or professional integrity to claim for itself a separate subject matter, its own curriculum, or a coherent body of knowledge. Indeed, the whole catalog of "how-tos" in J. Pierrepont's book might now be summarized, facetiously, by saying, "Get an MBA."

The enormous number of prospective managers who emerge from MBA programs around the country each year—over 75,000

---

[2]Peter Kann, *The Wall Street Journal*, January 9, 1989. The letter served as the lead article in the *Journal's* series, celebrating its 100th year of publication.

[3]This point about community standards and meaningful communication has many sources of support. Ludwig Wittgenstein's later work in the *Philosophical Investigations* speaks to the issue. Linguists and anthropologists since Whorf have recognized the importance of linguistic communities. Stanley Fish published a whimsical article on the subject, "Normal Circumstances, Literal Language, Direct Speech Acts, the Ordinary, the Everyday, the Obvious, What Goes Without Saying, and Other Special Cases," Paul Rabinow and William Sullivan, eds., *Interpretive Social Science: A Reader* (Berkeley: University of California Press, 1979), pp. 243–66.

at last count—provides ample evidence that the business world recognizes managers as a separable category of individuals with distinct skills, training, knowledge, and goals. Although some programs may do a better or worse job than others of preparing students to join the managerial community, all make some attempt to provide the knowledge necessary for students to take their places among more experienced practicing managers. As with all forms of professional training, whatever makes up the curriculum represents a collective judgment about the theories and skills that can be substituted for the knowledge gained from on-the-job experience.

More and more business educators express the hope that the managers they turn out will be educated in a broad range of ideas and concerns, some of which go far beyond what has become the traditional realm of business study. The business community, however, requires of these ambitious individuals the kind of competence that will allow them to carry the initiatives of American business into the next century. We hope that these two agendas are compatible. One can certainly become a successful manager even if one hasn't run the gauntlet of an MBA program, and one can still be managerially illiterate even if one has. Despite the increasing popularity of MBA programs, the pedigree means less than does the knowledge gained from these educational programs and how well a given manager puts it to use.

One way to understand the difficult balancing act involved in educating managers for business is simply to think of it as instilling a kind of managerial literacy. Plenty of successful managers may not know precisely how to finance a leveraged buyout, or how to calculate a weighted average cost of capital, or how to position a new product in the market. But our research suggests that few managers are wholly ignorant of the term and concepts that underlie these activities. Nor are they out of touch with what makes these activities useful or important. So that even when they don't do these things themselves, they can talk about them and participate in conversations that assume such knowledge. Often that conversational familiarity is enough to see that a job gets done, and done well.

LANGUAGE AND LITERACY

Putting a premium on the importance of language in the workplace connects the content of managerial literacy and the context of what managers spend most of their time doing. Studies have repeatedly shown that managers spend most of their time in conversation with their subordinates, their peers, and their superiors. Henry Mintzberg, in his classic study of what managers actually do, reported that "virtually every empirical study of managerial time allocation draws attention to the great proportion of time spent in verbal communication."[4] Estimates have varied from approximately 60 to 90 percent, but the practicing manager need not consult the findings of a study to corroborate these estimates. Observation can underscore the importance of these studies, which suggest that management not only depends on conversation but, in an important sense, management *is* conversation. All the activities regularly associated with management—setting goals, planning, organizing, fostering teamwork, coaching, evaluating, leading, inspiring, and controlling—regularly take place in the acts of listening and speaking.

Thinking of the practice of management in this way connects it intimately to the concept of literacy we have developed. On the simplest level, the more terms, idioms, and shared information managers have to draw on, the less often they will have to pretend to know something they don't know. We have all been in the compromising position of having to smile or nod our way through a conversation because some of the terms being used were unfamiliar. Very few people have either the courage or the composure to interrupt someone who is speaking in order to get a clarification or a definition of a term. And few people enjoy being interrupted merely to supply what they assume the listener already knows. Nearly all the diverse managers and executives interviewed for this book had a story or two to tell

---

[4]Henry Mintzberg, *The Nature of Managerial Work* (New York: Harper and Row, 1973), p. 222.

about the discomfort or embarrassment of such situations, on whichever side of the knowledge gap they stood.

Nobody wants to be embarrassed by a lack of knowledge in a particular area. Most people hesitate to admit that they don't know something that somebody else obviously finds important and appropriate to know. The missing knowledge needn't be particularly specialized or current to provoke anxiety or censure. The implicit judgment that one should know because of one's position or experience can be compelling enough.

Suppose, for instance, in the context of a conversation about particular stocks and the volatility of financial markets, one manager asks another, "Do you know the beta?" If the answer is "No," whether the second manager is merely uninformed of that particular statistic or wholly ignorant of what a *beta* refers to and bluffing his or her way through is not clear. In isolated cases, knowing something about a beta—a relative measure of the volatility, and therefore the riskiness, of a stock—may be of no practical significance. But the manager who asked the question is likely to avoid further conversation on the subject with someone who clearly doesn't have the conceptual framework to understand the terms in which the conversation might proceed. Worse, if the bluff worked, the first manager might never realize that the second didn't understand a critical part of the conversation.

There's no crime in bluffing one's way through a conversation by pretending to know things you don't, but neither is there anything particularly honorable in doing so. Most people, however, can read a poker face. Several managers told us they can tell when their peers or subordinates are feigning comprehension. Human faces have a way of glazing over when the brain is failing to process the information being given it. The generous view of this pretense to understanding sees it merely as benign illiteracy. And in many cases that's all it amounts to; some perfectly capable managers never deal with the side of business being discussed. But what about those instances in which the information *is* critical, where a lack of understanding deadens response in a way that curtails action? Is it benign to leave things undone, to miss important options, or to ignore clear signals because we've failed to educate ourselves properly?

The perception and tolerance of embarrassment varies from individual to individual, but at a level beyond embarrassment, there is the question of effective communication. Consider the following instance: several new managers have just joined a project group charged with bringing out a new product. The product manager takes the time to explain what's going on:

> I think we've nailed down the product concept. I'll handle the advertising copy and media scheduling. You'll work on the other elements of the marketing mix. A successful rollout using a pull strategy may make unanticipated demands on our production people. We've got to have some flexibility there. We've simply got to have plenty of product in the channels.

Here, even though the newcomers might understand the basic thrust of the explanation, important and useful information will be irretrievably lost if the hidden connections between, for instance, channels of distribution (one critical element of the marketing mix), a pull strategy, and production scheduling are not already established in the other managers' minds. Effective communication depends on sharing these background connections, which are triggered by the language common to managers.

It's a small leap from the level of communication to the level of managerial action. If a manager has to act on information communicated in a way that does not trigger the appropriate background connections and knowledge, the required action is likely to be off the mark or simply left undone. Successful problem-solving, in particular, depends on managers seeing the same problems and understanding them in roughly the same light. If, for example, one manager summarizes the problems she sees in a company by saying simply, "Well, it's a matrix organization," the phrase may do little to bring those problems into focus for another manager unfamiliar with how such organizations work. Even asking what the phrase means might not reveal the importance and utility of her observation unless the other manager can draw on a set of background associations and connections that parallel the speaker's.

The fundamental importance of such communication becomes clear when we recognize that the nature of various managerial problems depends partly on how we size them up, how we approach them, how we talk about them. The characteristic language of managers and executives who regularly face the daily pressures and problems of business thus traces their view of these problems and, to some extent, encodes the problems' potential solutions. This is where literacy of the sort we're interested in enters the picture. If an individual is unfamiliar with the phrases and ideas expressed in the language of practicing managers, he or she will not be able to understand critical conversations or recognize the same problems. The ability to listen, speak, and act coherently in the business community depends in large measure on just this familiarity. In the most practical sense, shared language and the associations and connections imbedded in it define the business community as a community by establishing its shared interests and perspectives. Managerial literacy means no more and no less than a working familiarity with the shared language of the business community.

That familiarity also implies the ability to distinguish important from unimportant issues. It may not mean that managers know how to solve all the problems they face. Literacy does not imply having all the answers. Indeed, the solutions to some problems are notoriously beyond the limits of managerial action. But a literate manager will often know where to get the appropriate information to tackle a problem or to make it more susceptible to solution. Simply knowing the limits of knowledge, recognizing the need for greater expertise, and imagining solutions (when necessary) beyond one's personal or immediate experiences are all steps in the right direction and marks of a literate manager.

By managerially literate we do not mean merely current or generally well read. One can read the front page of *The New York Times*, for instance, without being literate in those things that matter a great deal in business. Managers depend on their own shared knowledge, a set of connections and associations appreciably different from that of the general populace and culture. By the same token, being the first to be aware of the latest technological advances, the hottest new marketing techniques, the most talked-about scandal, and the newest management philosophy doesn't guarantee literacy either. Literacy depends upon *shared* knowledge. That knowledge is revealed in the language shared by the community of practicing managers. Managerial literacy thus depends on knowing the wide range of information reflected in the language of business.

MANAGERIAL LITERACY AND CULTURAL LITERACY

Both the notion of managerial literacy and the managerial literacy list that fulfills it grow out of fundamental work carried out by E. D. Hirsch, whose controversial bestseller, *Cultural Literacy: What Every American Needs to Know,* developed the groundwork for thinking about literacy in an entirely new way. Until Hirsch's work, literacy was essentially a remedial concept, a set of skills without which one could not read or write. The remedial aspect focused attention on lack of skills and accustomed us to hearing accounts of what happens in the absence of literacy. Most managers have heard the dramatic examples of the kind of trouble that illiteracy gets business into. The stories are by now legendary: the company that lost a million-dollar machine because some unfortunate machinist couldn't read the manual; the famous cases of misplaced decimals and commas costing companies hundreds of thousands of dollars. These incidents are profoundly regrettable and tell a sorry tale about the state of basic education in this country, but they do not illustrate the critical problem facing American business today. Indeed, losses due to remedial-level literacy are probably insignificant, though certainly dramatic, compared with those resulting from misunderstandings, missed opportunities, and higher-level *managerial* illiteracy.

Hirsch set the notion of literacy on its head by suggesting that the ultimate cure for problems of this sort was to stop thinking of literacy as a set of skills and treat it instead as a broad base of shared knowledge. Beyond the correct placement of commas, literacy entails sharing basic background knowledge that constitutes "culture." As Hirsch uses the term, *culture* is not at all meant to suggest anything remotely elitist (high culture) but rather to elevate common knowledge to new prominence. The kind of common sense or community that grows out of shared knowledge is partly what confers cultural identity on each member of that community. It is the range of associations connected to this knowledge that allows people to make sense to one another. In business, for instance, when someone uses a phrase like *sunk cost*, that person can be reasonably well assured it will be recognized by literate managers as something to do with accounting and finance, not maritime hazards. Hirsch demonstrated that factual knowledge and the shared meanings and associations that develop around this information—not abstract skills—provide the necessary preconditions for effective communication. The efficiencies often associated with skills can develop only later, after these conditions have been met.

In championing this common-sense, content-based notion of literacy, Hirsch developed an extensive list of factual knowledge that Americans need to know to be able to participate fully in their duties as responsible citizens. Defending this approach to literacy and the value of his list, Hirsch argues that "a misguided emphasis on skills has been the single most disastrous mistake of American schooling during the past forty years. An emphasis on skills coupled with a derogation of 'mere facts' is a cast of mind that distinguishes the thought-world of education professors from that of common sense."[5] Hirsch's list thus connects the ideals of community and common sense by stating that Americans need to share the broad range of background information, from *abolitionism* to *zodiac*, that literate Americans know. His arguments make it clear that we can easily lose our sense of cultural identity, our place in the community, if we don't recognize or can't tap this common knowledge. Cultural illiteracy thus leads to divisive and fragmented subcultures

[5]E. D. Hirsch, Jr., "The Primal Scene of Education," *The New York Review of Books*, 36, no. 3, pp. 29–35.

because it precludes a widely recognized community of values, traditions, knowledge, or shared perspective. Cultural literacy, on the other hand, exerts a galvanizing force because it constitutes and preserves shared background knowledge, while facilitating attempts to move beyond this knowledge.[6]

In building his arguments, Hirsch cites a number of examples of literacy from the business world, and one of his anecdotes helped to awaken our interest in exploring just what it is businesspeople ought to know:

> My father used to write business letters that alluded to Shakespeare. These allusions were effective for conveying complex messages to his associates, because, in his day, businesspeople could make such allusions with every expectation of being understood. For instance, in my father's commodity business, the timing of sales and purchases was all-important, and he would sometimes write or say to his colleagues, "There is a tide," without further elaboration. Those four words carried not only a lot of complex information, but also the persuasive force of a proverb. In addition to the basic practical meaning, "Act now!" what came across was a lot of implicit reasons why immediate action was important.[7]

The moral of this story, as Hirsch readily admits, is not that reading or citing Shakespeare will help one succeed in the business world. His point is both more general and more powerful: "The fact that middle-level executives no longer share

---

[6]Hirsch argues strenuously that the conservative notion of literacy does not interfere with either progress or radical change. Literacy is not meant to enshrine or canonize the particulars of cultural knowledge but rather to establish them as a threshold for adequate communication and cultural growth.

[7]E. D. Hirsch, Jr., *Cultural Literacy: What Every American Needs To Know* (Boston: Houghton Mifflin, 1987), p. 9. The Shakespearean allusion comes from *Julius Caesar,* Act 4, scene 3. The longer passage helps makes the elliptical reference clear:

> There is a tide in the affairs of men,
> Which taken at the flood, leads on to fortune;
> Omitted, all the voyage of their life
> Is bound in shallows and in miseries.
> On such a full sea are we now afloat,
> And we must take the current when it serves,
> Or lose our ventures.

literate background knowledge is a chief cause of their inability to communicate effectively."[8]

Although the view of the particulars of the language of business in this book differs markedly from Hirsch's, the authors share his view that language is crucial to management effectiveness. Hirsch is right to claim that a lack of shared knowledge impoverishes communication within organizations. We part company with Hirsch in identifying what that shared knowledge actually is. There can be no doubt that a sense of literacy in the broad cultural sense promotes better and richer communications between all people, from butchers to bankers. But although we may or may not privately regret the decline in the number of managers who read or cite Shakespeare, we are certainly not calling for a return to the days when business memoranda contained erudite and high-flown literary allusions. If business is likely to suffer—or is suffering—a crisis in communication, it is not because managers and executives can't register allusions to Shakespeare's plays, the Declaration of Independence, or the Gettysburg Address. The crisis is more internal to the business world, more peculiar to its mechanisms, initiatives, and idioms.

For better or worse, the business community exists largely on its own terms. Thus, while Hirsch's stories about cultural illiteracy should alarm us, perhaps we should be even more alarmed at the possibility that rising managers and executives lack essential information in their own professional precincts. Beyond a general need for cultural literacy, then, we see an urgent need for managerial literacy. In the absence of a shared sense of the knowledge that represents the common coin of business transactions, American enterprise will increasingly find itself without the means to carry out even the most rudimentary tasks.

---

[8]Hirsch, *Cultural Literacy,* pp. 9-10.

THE MANAGERIAL LITERACY LIST

We have, accordingly, defined what it means to be managerially literate by first isolating the body of working knowledge that American managers and executives regularly draw upon in the course of doing business. This working knowledge was then distilled in a list, assembled and tested over the past two years, of the shared language that adheres to and shapes the community of practicing managers and executives. The list of items represents this core knowledge, the ideas and information that are widely shared by managers in businesses across the country and that they consider important to their work. The list thus reflects a *de facto* community of managers and interests and reveals the language in which its members can communicate easily and effectively with one another. It is primarily this latter characteristic that should make the list important to practicing managers and executives, as well as to those who aspire to management positions and responsibilities.

The creation and testing of the list had to be particularly sensitive to the issues of currency and specificity. Business is changing rapidly. Keeping up with a shifting core of critical information and knowledge poses obvious problems. What's worse, the language that carries these concepts and ideas often has a very short half-life. Splashy and faddish ideas may or may not endure long after they hit the market. Some never achieve widespread currency; some rise and fade too quickly to make much of an impression. How much of this sort of information a manager must know—where to draw the line—presented a practical puzzle.

We looked for language that was current but captured enduring business concerns. Some business language has gone out of fashion, although the concern remains intact in an alternate phrase. The tag, *customer's man,* for example, has become an archaic (still used, but not necessarily or widely understood) term for a *registered representative* or broker. Almost everyone still knows the term *greenbacks,* which has an illustrious popular and economic history, but few still use it to denote our common legal tender. Sometimes a concept goes out of currency with the language: we don't hear many managers talking anymore about *therbligs,* a term for a unit of work that came into use in the 1940s. Sometimes a concept comes into currency with the language, as in new coinages like *greenmail* or *gray market.* How long-lasting and how powerful such language may be in the managerial community is not always clear. Already, for instance, we've seen that managers don't think that recognition of the name *Ivan Boesky* is very important; but *insider trading* is still a generally understood, widely recognized, and significant concept.

Perhaps a greater challenge than meeting the need for currency was establishing the appropriate level of detail. An important concern in shaping the list was not to become too general or too specific, especially given the differences in the degree of specialization among practicing managers. Most accountants, for instance, know particular FASB rules, some of which clearly bear on day-to-day business operations. The proverbial man on the street has never heard of FASB (Financial Accounting Standards Board). Most managers, however, while they may know little about particular rules, do know what FASB stands for, know that it is the rule-making body for the accounting profession, and know how to use it intelligibly in a conversation with other managers. *FASB* goes on the list because it evokes precisely these things among most managers who do not need to know more specific detail. *Advertising,* on the other hand, was left off because the word carries only a general set of widely recognized associations (not specific to managers).

The development of the list and the wrestling with these judgments provided the researchers with some insights into how managers store and use information. Those insights confirm the crucial importance for managers and executives throughout organizations of being able to speak one another's language. All the managers and executives interviewed in the process of putting together and shaping the list had something to say about how communication in organizations gets held up by differing literacy levels. Not only do people in operations, for example, have trouble talking to people in marketing, but even within the functional areas, varying degrees of literacy may garble otherwise clear and efficient communication. Further up the organizational ladder, senior executives and CEOs have wondered why it's so difficult to make their "vision" understood throughout the corporation.

The managerial literacy list represents the core working knowledge that managers in the business community regularly draw upon in their day-to-day transactions. It contains those concepts, names, phrases, dates, idioms, and abbreviations that practicing managers have agreed are central to their work. Of course, not every item is central to every manager, but the total represents the knowledge necessary to support the managerial community's business interests and activities. Moreover, the list works because every element in it will evoke a whole range of associations to the managerially literate, so that any one item— *cost of capital,* for example—immediately calls up related bits of information, both on and off the list. Hirsch calls such a web of associations a *schema,* which he says "functions as a unified system of background relationships whose visible parts stand for the rest of the schema."[9] Thus, *advertising copy,* for instance, can evoke a whole matrix of relationships, something like the one shown in Figure 1–1:

FIGURE 1–1
Matrix of Relationships Evoked by Sample Terms

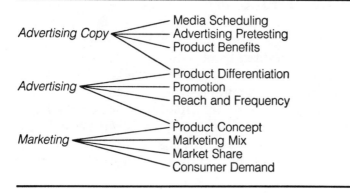

---

[9]Hirsch, *Cultural Literacy,* p. 54.

The diagram in Figure 1–1 can't represent the complexity of the recall or retrieval process. But something of these deeper connections and cross-connections are part of the apparatus of meaning when literate managers communicate. As Hirsch points out, "One element of a schema represents many other subterranean elements, allowing us to deploy that one surface element as though the whole complex schema were a single item."[10] Individual items on the literacy list should, therefore, be thought of as occasions for retrieving a larger, more comprehensive, cross-referenced web of associations. In this way, literacy not only involves the recognition of individual items, but also implies the successful retrieval of this deeper grid of meanings and connections.

It is virtually impossible to specify how detailed these grids must be to guarantee that someone really knows any given item. Part of the value of the list as a whole is to provide some of the more important cross-connections. Managers and executives need not know any individual item in great detail because the list itself helps to establish these complex connections. Literate managers and executives draw on these connections all the time, consciously or not, because the grids support a clear pattern of understanding and provide the associations to motivate appropriate action.

THE LIMITS OF LITERACY

Managerial literacy is an inherently enabling concept, and the list is meant to provide managers with the means to function effectively in an environment that gets more bewildering and more glutted with new information every day. In calling attention to the importance of basic information, the literacy list is designed to stabilize this knowledge, to keep it from being lost to a despairing posterity. Cynics might maintain, however, that the sheer diversity and ethnic plurality of American culture

---

[10]Hirsch, *Cultural Literacy*, p. 57.

argues against the formation of any such list, either in the general realm of culture or in the more specific domain of business. But what lies behind this objection is precisely the tendency to regard our culture and the business community as a random, fragmented collection of parts, not as a true community. To a large extent, the list itself should serve as a partial antidote to this view.

In the business world, the cynical viewpoint finds some justification in the fragmented plurality of industry traditions and myths, corporate cultures, and company-specific languages. There is nothing inherently insidious about the fact that the world of business is composed of many languages, each peculiar to its area and organization. Corporate plurality, like ethnic plurality, can lay claims to its own set of terms, concepts, and idioms. But these various languages only imperfectly intersect: no one industry or corporation, no one manager or executive, can make any communal claims about a particular language. We have already argued that this lack of intersection is the most important reason why people in different industries often find it so difficult to understand one another. Our work has suggested that, despite these differences, the business community not only wants to recognize itself as a community, but needs to do so. Managerial literacy can thus be best appreciated as a familiarity with the language most common to American corporate cultures. It represents the vocabulary one must know to gain access to those cultures, to speak the language they collectively speak.

The central problem with defining the vocabulary that binds the business community together is that it automatically excludes highly technical and specialized languages that overlap to some extent with the more broadly shared ideas and information. Setting the limits may seem arbitrary. We certainly had to reckon with the fact that the language that adheres to particular fields—computer technology, for instance—can be far too specialized to serve the broader community. Indeed, specialized languages, like those of individual companies, are useful and necessary to the adequate functioning of the specialized businesses that use them. But they do not constitute a good benchmark for literacy.

Although the list might have been doubled or tripled in order to give more due to different areas of expertise, the aim was to isolate a set of terms that is cross-functional, reasonably general, and current. The present list therefore compresses and consolidates information and should be considered as representing a minimum standard. Familiarity with 80 percent of the items on it represents the threshold of literacy. This standard doesn't mean you cannot succeed as a manager if you can identify only 75 percent. Knowing less than 80 percent does mean that the risk of missing important elements of business conversations *without knowing you're missing them* is greater than you should be willing to accept.

In the course of testing and verifying the list, we found that managers and executives do agree on the knowledge that ought to be their mutual provenance. We simply supplied the context and the occasion for these people to speak to the issue of what managers know. The list describes their judgments. At some point, of course, it is difficult to separate what managers *do* know from what they *ought to* know. In formulating and presenting the list, we are not only excluding a lot of very specific language but also suggesting a prescriptive formula for what counts as necessary to literacy.

The difference between a descriptive list and a prescriptive one is hard to maintain. It is virtually impossible to create any list that doesn't have some prescription in it. Even the proverbial laundry list carries with it an implied prescription for action. In promulgating the idea of literacy as a community standard, we have tried to dissolve the distinction. What many managers *do* know implicitly contains a message for other managers: they must be familiar with at least this knowledge if they hope to be able to talk together and depend on each other's understanding and cooperation.

Clearly, however, managerial literacy is not a magic wand that managers can wave over a corporation to increase its profits. The list is not a panacea. Neither is it a saber with which they can cut the competition down to size. It is, however, the necessary condition for doing either of these things. Without a high degree of familiarity with at least a core of business knowledge, one will have difficulty being a team player, a sharp-sighted manager, or a responsible executive. Knowledge can temper ambition by restoring a sense of relative stability and cooperation to managers who have to function in a chaotic and competitive world. Literacy provides the basis and opportunity for creating order out of chaos by allowing managers to build on a core of knowledge, understanding, and agreement.

One may succeed in spite of one's ignorance but never because of it. Just as studies have found a correlation between the size of a working vocabulary and success in a chosen profession, so too we have found a connection between managerial literacy and managerial prowess. The list itself represents the more enabling knowledge implicit in it. The items are not a series of magical words for success, but knowing them makes successful action possible by connecting managers to a rich network of meanings beyond the particular elements that make up the ongoing conversation of the business community. There is nothing mysterious about this. When a word or term evokes a cluster of associations and deeper background knowledge, we suddenly realize that we know more than we had imagined, and new options become available. That is the basis of literacy. The point, therefore, is not merely to limit oneself to identifying the items on the list but to pay attention to the kinds of associations and patterns of connection that each item can evoke.

BEYOND LITERACY

We would be foolish to predict the scope, speed, or direction of the coming changes in the business world. American business is facing competition it has never known before, seeing opportunities it has never recognized before, and needing cooperation it has never required before. Executives must broaden their thinking and restructure some of their most cherished notions of doing business in order to respond to global opportunities and global complexities. To do so, they need, at a minimum, to recognize the centrality of language and communication in business.

Businesspeople must communicate, and they must communicate as efficiently and as powerfully as possible. In our terms, this means possessing a high degree of managerial literacy—a rich, precise, and suggestive vocabulary for getting one's own ideas across and for listening intelligently to the ideas of others. Our list captures the essence of such a vocabulary, but by no means does it forever fix its outer limits. By identifying the core of managerial literacy, we offer a conservative estimate of the basic information needed to enter skillfully and confidently into the business conversations that figure so prominently in a manager's daily life. The kind of literacy we have mapped gets managers back to the basics so that they can, if they have the energy and the imagination, go beyond them.

By defining what it means to be managerially literate, we seek to provide a useful benchmark for a managerial community facing some of the toughest and most pressing problems of recent decades. Literacy can ensure full participation in the business community at large, a community that has a growing stake in its own professional fluency. The managerial literacy list can, at the very least, act as a self-check on a manager's literacy level within particular areas of specialization and, more importantly, across those areas. The list thus both poses a challenge and offers hope for those who wish to remain current in their chosen fields and for those who might wish to assess how much they know about the key terms and concepts peculiar to their profession as a whole. Simply knowing many of these core terms will go a long way toward making one a better participant in the wide range of transactions and conversations that constitute managerial activity.

Beyond this commonsense appreciation of the practical and timely importance of managerial literacy lies a vision of future literacy, the contours of the language that businesspeople will use in the next century. Where will the terms, ideas, and idioms that form this language come from? Everywhere. Language from other cultures, language from other communities of interest (science and technology, for example), as well as language from the past will continue to enter and shape our future business language. Just as, for example, the word *weekend* has entered almost every major language in the world, bringing with it some of the American sense of what makes it different from a week, new language will shape and reshape managerial conversations. With this language will come new ideas, new patterns of connection, and a new managerial literacy.

Managerial literacy, however, is an essentially conservative notion: a benchmark is an explicit standard. The managerial literacy list is composed of what managers and executives need to know *now* to thrive in the business community. But the concept of literacy that we have outlined here will serve managers well for years to come. In this spirit we offer the managerial literacy list as both a strong bulwark against senseless drift and a powerful catalyst for meaningful change.

CHAPTER 2

CRAFTING THE MANAGERIAL LITERACY LIST

Crafting the managerial literacy list took as much art as it did science. The most interesting aspects of the project were usually connected to conversations with groups of managers and individual executives at various stages of the list's development. We regularly invited managers to comment on what we were doing and to lend their particular expertise to our work. Although these comments often reflected isolated, individual perspectives on the list and on literacy, they added up over time and created a weighty sense of what the contribution of the list and the ideas behind it amounted to. One manager, a foreign national who works for Unilever, a large multinational corporation, elegantly summed up the value of the list, after examining a late draft:

> I was aware that there was something like a fundamental bank of knowledge, which was necessary to know. But, I had never thought of its significance or the need to see its elements. The list brought that into very sharp focus.

While the whole list, even in its half-formed stages, clarified for many the logic of literacy and the need to isolate basic knowledge, putting it together raised issues that were less clear-cut.

CRAFTING THE RIGHT LIST

Any management textbook can provide a list of some words, phrases, and concepts important to managers. But our list needed to cut across narrow fields and disciplines, to bridge formal and informal knowledge, to be comprehensive, current, and, to whatever extent possible, idiomatic. The list needed to represent the kind of language that managers could use in daily conversations without needing to explain what they meant.

Most managers implicitly assume that this mutual understanding is in place when they talk about important ideas and issues, but often it is not. Although literacy is an attempt to reveal and close the gaps that make the transmission of meaning difficult at best, we could not simply collect the many instances of breakdown or success. We needed *both* if we were to capture the assumed background knowledge needed to communicate well. Our methodology therefore needed to enable managers to listen and judge in our places for expressions critical to the success or failure of communication—and then to give us the benefit of their experience.

Our biggest responsibility was to convey to these managers a clear sense of what to "listen for" in judging these expressions. Instead of providing guidelines, we provided a preliminary list that we hoped would be comprehensive enough for managers to simply exclude those items that their experience told them were not central enough, not current enough, not widespread enough, or not conversational enough to warrant inclusion on the final literacy list. Since it was unlikely that the initial list included everything that managers might actually hear in their business dealings, or the knowledge that makes that language important, we had to allow for potential new inclusions at every stage. Until the very end, the process of crafting the list thus tugged us in two directions at once and forced us to make regular adjustments in our editing.

WORDS, WORDS, WORDS

The difficulties inherent in this process were compounded by the problems of dealing with language, the difficulties of working with an inherently diverse managerial community, and the tedious artificiality of using surveys. The sheer size of the preliminary list made it difficult to see overlaps and duplications. Indeed, early discussions with selected managers often involved substituting a single item for several alternatives that appeared on the preliminary list in different places. Our methods, moreover, needed to take into account that the items on the final list would stand *cumulatively* for the knowledge that literate managers share. Surveys force managers to judge individual items one-by-one. Cumulative averages of the scores for each item would finally allow us to rank order the items simply on their importance to the survey community. But it was clear from the outset that the judgment of the whole had to affect the scoring of the parts.

After one develops the initial list and the guidelines from which to select the items for the final list, the analysis can proceed in a reasonably orderly and systematic way. The entries can be evaluated on the basis of overall consensus about their importance and appropriateness to the standard. But this process presents a central conceptual puzzle. When managers and executives are asked to choose among entries, they are actually validating choices already made:

> The real problem is therefore not in the analysis of the corpus but in the principles for choosing the corpus in the first place. This problem cannot be solved by any amount of technical expertise.[1]

Being aware of this problem from the beginning clarified our responsibilities, since the process of crafting the list necessarily involved value judgments as well as inductive observations and deductive reasoning.

Inasmuch as the list works to define a community, members of that community must help to define the list. Any manager surveyed about the list becomes, statistically speaking, a member of that community and helps to shape its standards and its language. But statistics cannot replace the important shaping

---

[1]E. D. Hirsch, in July 1988 conversation (in Charlottesville, Virginia) with the authors about the difficulties and responsibilities of building such lists, talked about this puzzle as, "the problem of the corpus." It is well known in linguistic circles.

values involved in defining the knowledge and the community with which we were concerned. Both the choice of managers and the original choice of material for the list determined its ultimate shape. Over the course of the project we talked to or surveyed over 500 managers and executives, from middle managers to CEOs, representing a broad cross-section of industries and organizations. Their insights as well as their individual decisions, the principles of judgment that guided their evaluations, and their choices for inclusions and exclusions were finally as important to us as any statistics they yielded.

DISCOVERING THE LIMITS OF THE LIST

After threading our way through the maze of language we sought to examine, we had to establish the threshold level of literacy. To avoid being arbitrary, we had to look closely at the relation between the process of producing the list and the final product. While managers' collective judgments about the importance of individual items allowed us to pare down the list with confidence, these judgments did not tell us where to establish a final limit to the size of the list. We had to work on the assumption that the list would approach its final size and shape when we started having trouble throwing off items—for statistical, and other, reasons. The notion of managerial literacy involved isolating important shared knowledge, but there is no *predetermined* means for discovering the threshold limit of literacy.

We gradually discovered this limit by submitting the working list to the scrutiny of a succession of managers and executives who were asked to make cuts and suggest additions or alternatives. The items were arrayed in different sequences, but to permit us to see how the items grouped themselves in successive testings and revisions, only one question was asked about all the items. The respondents thus tied their judgments to a single notion—the importance of each item to managerial literacy. This focus allowed us to figure out the statistical relation between gaps and overlaps in the percentage of items managers knew.

Given these initial concerns and constraints, no one method for constructing the literacy list recommended itself. Constructing the managerial literacy list demanded a remarkable amount of to and fro movement. Indeed, the process of iteration—of going over the list again and again, looking at it from slightly different angles, and editing it with the guidance of several different groups of managers—was the single most important method used in its construction. The process was long and rigorous and as systematic as is possible when dealing with something as elusive as knowledge and as dynamic as language.

GENERATING THE LIST

Generating an initial, "all-inclusive" list, a list containing many items that we thought to be overly specific or overly general, was clearly the first step; most of the subsequent work would entail thinning out the list. All subsequent steps in the process would therefore involve the basic judgment of whether to include or exclude an item. Our managerial populations would shape the list by their decisions at each stage. Their choices guided us to a final list of less than half the number of original entries, even though we built in safeguards at every stage so that previously excluded materials could be ransomed and reincluded. The initial list was compiled with the help of a panel of consultants consisting of business educators, middle managers, and upper-level executives. This panel offered recommendations for inclusions on the literacy list. In follow-up interviews, we went through their recommendations, probing for logic, consistency, and omissions. To these recommendations, we added language from an informal content analysis of leading business periodicals and newspapers including *The Wall Street Journal, Business Week, Harvard Business Review,* and the business pages of *The New York Times.* By then many of the terms that jumped out at us from these pages were already on the list, but we discovered some commonly used terms that had escaped our notice. At the end of this initial stage of the process, the list bulked out at nearly 2,500 items.[2]

DRAWING IN THE BOUNDARIES: EDITING AND TESTING THE LIST

After generating an all-inclusive list, we were faced with the tasks of editing and testing it. Somewhere in this bulky list was the core of managerial literacy, a list that best represented what practicing managers and executives find important to know. Editing and testing the list were interdependent activities and produced a continuous rhythm of vision and revision. This iterative method, the task of going over the list and immersing it in more and more clarifying solutions, engaged us in regular dialogue with those managers who were examining the list. From the earliest respondents, we learned just how bulky and imprecise our initial list had become, how interlarded with duplications, solecisms, and overlapping terms. Our later respondents, whom we called upon to examine the pared-down list, helped identify and weed out overly technical and general terms, dated expressions, and trendy catchphrases.

The elimination of the various duplications and imprecisions that had collected early on allowed each item on the later list to receive independent evaluation. It was difficult at first for respondents to deal with the sheer size and relative shapelessness of the list. The idea of the literacy list suggested that the boundaries within which managers would not have to explain their use of terms could be mapped on the basic dimensions of currency and specificity. Figure 2–1 shows how a sample of items from the preliminary list might array themselves on these dimensions. The boundaries at either end of these two dimensions represent the cutoff points beyond which the items appeared too new or too dated, too general or too specialized.

---

[2]If, as Hirsch claims, American culture can be captured in a list of 5,000 items, it was reasonable to suppose that managerial literacy would comprise a substantially smaller set of items.

FIGURE 2–1
Sample Items Mapped According to Currency and Specificity

SPECIALIZED

Therblig   psychographics
                                            Eurobond

                       demographics

                                  J-I-T

D
A   Strategic   N
T   Planning   LBO   E
E   W
D

    economies
    of scale

                              Ivan
                              Boesky

       monopoly

          law of supply & demand

GENERAL

Our early respondents, however, found it hard to see these
dimensions clearly. The sheer profusion of entries raised questions about large clusters of items and undercut the confidence
that managers had in their particular judgments. For example,
the initial list had the entries *MRP* and *Material Requirements
Planning.*The judgment of which of the two forms best represented common managerial parlance clouded the judgment of
whether the concept behind both was important enough to
retain either. Similarly, along the other dimension, the entries
J-I-T and *just-in-time* raised the problem of newer coinages.

Some managers knew only the whole phrase, *just-in-time;* many others referred to the concept in its abbreviated form.

Months of testing and editing resolved most of these conceptual problems, allowed us to prune and graft entries, and thus made it easier for managers to grasp and evaluate the list. As items dropped from the initial list or were fused with other items, the basic contours and dimensions of managerial literacy began to emerge, clarifying for managers the decisions they had to make. These basic dimensions then served as the backdrop against which to judge each item's importance. They became for us central principles for continued editing.

The New and the Dated

It was not always easy to judge which words or phrases are currently in favor, just out of favor, or just coming into favor. Some language moves meteorically through the business world and burns itself up within a few months. Other pieces of language remain in place, joining with additional language to form constellations. It is impossible to predict these movements with unerring accuracy, and so we cut only those terms that had clearly become outdated, and we left all the marginal cases on the list for later groups of managers to evaluate. Our preliminary testing quickly determined, for example, that *quality assurance* has now replaced *quality control,* and most *comptrollers* are now called *controllers. CIO* (Chief Information Officer), on the other hand, is just coming around the corner, gaining currency, but not enough to be included on the list as a term managers recognize and find important.

The Specialized and the General

If the words or concepts in question appeared primarily within the confines of a textbook, then they usually fared poorly with managers and were removed from the list. Items that managers simply didn't recognize had to be retained on the list at this time, even though they might have been too specialized. But items that represented overly specialized knowledge, as judged by managers who knew this material, were summarily lopped off. The final list, therefore, was less likely to reflect only the special vocabulary one can learn in undergraduate or graduate business programs than to reflect what one has retained and found of continuing importance in one's job. Here are some terms that managers found either too technical or too specialized to pass muster:

free carry
reciprocal interdependence
lagged variable
continuous probe function
normlessness
conversion parity
TIGR
nonnegativity

On the other side of the spectrum were the terms that were thought to be overly general. These terms were eliminated because they could be used in everyday conversations by average Americans. Such entries, which might still seem business-related in a broad sense, nevertheless fail to capture the special character of managerial language. The following items provide clear examples of such language:

check register
manager
secretary
barter
voucher
Treasury Department
population
advertising
usury

Also in this category were terms associated with personal taxation and savings. *IRA, itemized deductions, personal exemp-*

tions, tax returns, and taxable income, certainly do pertain to business, but they are either too generally understood or too limited to nonprofessional, personal life to belong on a managerial literacy list.

This guideline became difficult to follow, however, as the list got pared down to a core, because as the boundaries of the list drew tighter around its most basic elements, it also became more rigorously business-specific. *Greenback,* for example, was late in being edited from the list. Even though the term still appears occasionally in the pages of *The Wall Street Journal,* it is relatively dated and generally connected to a world not specifically associated with managerial expertise.

Management Focus Groups

In our first round of interviews, we enlisted managers from a two-week general management seminar. These upper-middle managers represented a broad cross section of industries and management specialties. Twenty-four managers agreed to examine an alphabetized form of the initial list and to exclude any items that they thought were not critical to managerial literacy. We then conducted three eight-person focus groups and went through the entire list, item by item, discussing the respondents' rationale for recommending or deleting items. These discussions allowed us to consolidate many items and eliminate terms that were clearly unimportant to all the participants. The focus groups gave us a chance to look more closely at the boundaries of the list and to see more easily the principles of exclusion for those items too specialized or too generic, too faddish or too archaic, to remain on the list. At the end of this part of the process, the number of items on the list hovered around 1,500.

This initial set of interviews confirmed that we were on the right track. We nevertheless understood that the list required substantial editing to get it to the point where managers could review it without stumbling across a lot of superfluous terms. But the most important results of the focus groups were in allowing us to purge the list of all its duplications, to consolidate

items, and to consider the kind of questions we could ask
managers in order to establish the benchmark for their literacy.

Two Rules of Thumb

Two related rules of thumb for shaping the list thus emerged
from these focus groups. These rules served as guidelines for
purging the list of a host of duplications and overlapping terms.
At times, this sort of consolidating and thinning out produced
lively disputes and had us debating which of two or three nearly
synonymous entries to include on the list. As an intellectual
exercise, this kind of semantic melding felt like splitting hairs
in reverse.

The Duplication Rule

The early list contained dozens of terms whose meanings were
either interchangeable or overlapping. In the former category,
for instance, the list contained twins such as *variable work shifts*
and *flextime*. In the latter category, proper names kept popping
up because these names are sometimes used almost synony-
mously with concepts or terms associated with them. Consider
Reagan, Reaganomics, and *supply-side economics.* Or *Karl
Marx, Marxism,* and *communism.* Or *Adam Smith,* the *Wealth of
Nations,* and the *Invisible Hand.* In some cases, name recognition is a kind of abbreviation for the concept or the theory
associated with it. In other cases, the reverse is true. Names can
be important in and of themselves, but they can also pass in and
out of fashion rather quickly. Names, we found—even names of
famous entrepreneurs—were generally so unpopular with our
survey populations that we later took all of them off the list.
This decision also allowed us to keep the list from having the
appearance of a popularity contest.

The Umbrella Rule

Many terms and expressions on the initial list didn't quite
overlap, yet they were so closely associated that it made sense to
find the one term that best represented the others. The trick was
to find a single term to act as an umbrella for those it must cover.
This also raised issues about the network of related associations

each term triggered. Finding the appropriate umbrella term often involved tracking down experts in the field familiar with the array of terms in question or hashing out the various possibilities with managers. We also had to consider which term in the array of possible terms managers used most consistently.

Many groups of items required consolidation according to this rule of thumb. Here are a few examples:

- Advertising, advertising copy, advertising copy testing, advertising frequency, advertising pretesting;
- Brand, brand loyalty, brand management, brand name, brand switching, umbrella brand;
- Capital gains (and losses), capital gains tax;
- Cost control, cost containment, cost cutting, cost process, cost reporting, cost systems, costing;
- Quality, quality assurance, quality circles, quality control, quality of design, quality of performance, quality of service, total quality;
- Market share, share of market;
- BCG matrix, cash cow, dog, rising star, problem child;
- Quantity theory of money, monetarism, M1, money supply;
- Segment, segmentation, market segmentation;
- Stockout costs, cost of missed sales;
- S&P, Standard & Poors, S&P 500.

Many times, as in some of the above examples, discrete differences had to be respected, and closely related items remain on the final list. At first, the entries *strategic planning, long-range planning, short-range planning, planning, plans, corporate strategy,* and *competitive strategy* all appeared on the list. Although each was, in and of itself, important to many managers, some of the items formed equally important clusters. Other items, however, clearly conjured up such distinct sets of associations that they could not be reasonably subsumed by alternate terms. Partial redundancy was possible, but every effort was made to maintain the integrity of individual items.

There were a surprising number of cases in which the items in question commanded this sort of consideration. Except for obvious calls, however, we left large clusters of terms on the list and let managers decide which terms ought to enjoy primacy. As a result of early testing and editing—and the application of these two basic rules—the original list slimmed down considerably. During this stage, the initial list underwent its single most substantial reduction. Although this reduction made the list much less cumbersome and repetitive, the list was not the honed instrument we wanted to send out as a national survey, and we were fortunate to have a group of managers and executives on hand to help us make a final pass at the preliminary list.

Executive Program Survey

At this stage, we were interested not only in reducing the list even further but also in making sure we would be asking the right question of our final survey population. To help us accomplish both goals, we recruited a representative sample of upper-level American and international managers attending a six-week residential executive program. We asked half the respondents to rate the items according to their *familiarity,* and the other half to assess the *importance* of each item. Not surprisingly, the mean familiarity rating was substantially higher than was the mean rating for importance, suggesting that many items that managers knew well were nevertheless unimportant to them.[3] An analysis of means allowed us to eliminate some items, although we took the statistics at this point as recommendations for editing, not as rationales for automatic inclusion or exclusion.

National Management Sample

After six months of interviews, focus groups, and preliminary testing, the list was sufficiently shaped and edited to mail out as

---

[3]A regression between familiarity and importance ratings indicated that the measures were not independent and that the perceptions of importance were highly correlated with familiarity.

a nationwide survey. Once the final list was established, managers would have to assess their familiarity with the items in measuring their literacy. But in creating this list, asking practicing managers to rate their familiarity with each item on the list would tell us what they knew, not how important a given term or word might be for their daily business transactions. As our earlier work suggested, businesspeople know a lot more than they use or find important. Since believing a term is important implies familiarity with it, and since we wanted managers and executives to define, de facto, their own language community, the single question for rating the items on the survey had to concern importance.

We sent out the survey to hundreds of managers and executives from a broad cross section of industries, from heavy manufacturing to consumer products to banking and financial services. Most of our respondents were middle managers. The results of this survey allowed us to make our final editorial decisions, which involved cutting the bottom 10 percent of the remaining items from the list. That cut eliminated all the items receiving particularly low scores.

We might have edited beyond this point, but more severe cuts would have made it difficult to represent adequately all the functional areas of business. Our early testing and editing had already cut the list roughly in half. Cutting it further meant grossly underrepresenting several areas. Such cuts, moreover, would have trivialized the concept of literacy by producing a list of only those terms with which all managers could not help but be familiar. The list needed to represent the entire range of business activities that managers should come to know, not merely parrot back to them what they already knew.

Removing only 10 percent made sense, too, because the importance ratings formed a normal distribution. The clear statistical cutoffs occurred at the top and the bottom 10 percent. Although for many managers the items just above the bottom 10 percent cutoff were not indispensable, for some they were clearly worth preserving. Of course, we could have kept pruning from the bottom, but then we would always have to face the question of where to stop. After the 10 percent cutoff, the remaining items on the list were statistically "of a piece."

The Top 10 Percent

On the other side of the spectrum were the words that rated in the top 10 percent (see Figure 2–2). Although these items are highly rated, they do not constitute the bare essentials of literacy. Only the entire managerial literacy list can give full due to the breadth and depth of connections that inform business life. The items within the top 10 percent do not differ in kind from the rest of the list. They do, however, represent what a broad cross section of managers and executives felt were among the most important and vital terms, concepts, and idioms in their business lives.

FIGURE 2–2
The Managerial Literacy List: Top Ten Percent

accounting systems	contract
accounts payable and receivable	corporate culture
acquisition	corporate image
assets	corporate mission
balance sheet	corporate strategy
board of directors	cost
bonus plan	cost allocation
bottom line	cost center
brand loyalty	cost containment
breakeven analysis	cost of capital
budget variance	cost-benefit analysis
budgeting	database
business cycle	debit
capacity planning	decentralized organization
capital	demographics
capital expenditure	depreciation
capitalism	distribution channels
cash flow	diversification
cash management	divestiture
centralized organization	divisional structure
CEO	DP (data processing)
competition	economies of scale
competitive advantage	equity
competitive strategy	executive summary
competitiveness	expense budget
conflict of interest	financial analysis

FIGURE 2–2
Continued

fiscal year	present value
fixed asset	price elasticity
fixed cost	price sensitivity
focus group	product differentiation
gross income	product innovation
incentive compensation	Product Life Cycle (PLC)
incremental cost	product manager
indirect cost	product quality
inflation	productivity
interest rate	profit
inventory	profit center
job satisfaction	profit sharing
joint venture	profitability ratios
law of supply and demand	projected cost
leadership style	quality assurance
learning curve	resource allocation
liabilities	restructuring
long-range (and short-range) planning	return on capital
management development	ROI (return on investment)
market demand	sales force
market expansion	sales forecasting
market penetration	sales mix
market potential	sales promotion
marketing mix	sales representative
marketing research	sampling
marketing strategy	segmentation
mature industry	sensitivity analysis
merger	standard deviation
MIS (management information systems)	start-up costs
motivation	strategic planning
net income	survey population
net worth	takeover target
niche strategy	target market
operating income	task force
organizational chart	team building
organizational structure	test market
overhead	top-down communication
P&L (profit and loss)	turnover
participative management	unit cost
PC	value added
policies and procedures	variable cost
positioning	working capital
PR (public relations)	

CHARACTERISTICS OF THE MANAGERIAL LITERACY LIST

The final list represents a good benchmark for the language that managers use to talk to one another and to function effectively in the workplace. There are 1,200 items on the list. That number is happily random in the sense that we set no predetermined limit on the final size of the list. We arrived at this number by explaining the dimensions of literacy to managers and executives and then asking them to exclude inappropriate items and add other appropriate ones. The resulting list is arguably less certain at its margins than at its core. As new ideas and expressions gain currency and older ones fade, the contents of the list will change. Similarly, along another dimension, managers will see some items as more or less central to their experience and their jobs. It should be useful, therefore, to point out some broad characteristics of the list and its contents. We wanted to suggest in advance a few ways of seeing what's on the list, what's not on it, and how the list as a whole fits into the broader patterns of language and culture.

Managerial Literacy and General Knowledge

General literacy is concerned with extensive cultural knowledge and vocabulary. Managerial literacy puts a premium on the language that lies within the confines of the list. That language enables managers to *manage by conversation*. There is, however, a far broader world of knowledge pertinent to business that doesn't appear on the list. That general cultural knowledge underlies and affirms the place of business enterprise in our society. Without this broad foundation, it would be especially difficult to become managerially literate. Managerial literacy therefore relies to some extent on a broader literacy.

Indeed, much of the language on the literacy list may appear technical from the perspective of nonmanagers, even though the average American citizen is each year called upon to know an increasing number of business-related terms. James Kett recently noted that "the deregulation of financial institutions by the federal government, the vast growth of pension funds within the last twenty years, and recent changes in the federal tax code have raised the threshold of financial knowledge for Americans."[4] As business becomes more a part of American culture, business language figures more prominently in the range of information an American must know to be considered broadly literate. Because business and economic knowledge has become more important for Americans, a larger corner of the map of managerial literacy overlaps with the map of general literacy. Almost any American citizen—not simply managers—can therefore see a number of familiar items on the literacy list. What separates managerial literacy from general, cultural literacy is the large percentage of terms and concepts associated with the former with which an average American is *not* familiar.

Because the language central to managerial conversations will change, as all language changes over time, managers also need to be aware of the kind of language that was never under consideration for inclusion on the managerial literacy list but that still exerts a subtle pressure on the list's contents. After all, as the language of other fields (such as those connected to the humanities, for instance) gains a hearing and starts to enjoy greater currency, it will no doubt become increasingly integrated into the language of business. The changing place of accounting language offers an instructive illustration. The language of accounting once enjoyed centrality in the world of business and in the domain of business education. Our results indicate that accounting is now one among many languages found to be important to business, and it has apparently lost some of the unchallenged dominion it once had over other fields and other ways of speaking and thinking

Balance across Disciplines and Functions

The managerial literacy list generally shows a balance across functions, from marketing and operations to legal and policy issues. We kept track of the provenance of each item so that we

[4]James Kett, *The Dictionary of Cultural Literacy* (Boston: Houghton Mifflin Company, 1988), p. 413.

could see how various disciplines and functional areas were represented on the final list. Many items, of course, can be put comfortably under more than one rubric, but most could be assigned to a particular category without doing them a disservice. Items associated directly with the primary functional areas of business—marketing, finance, and operations—accounted for about 35 percent of the items on the list. Items associated with the accounting and reporting functions—accounting, statistics, and MIS—contributed about 25 percent. Items associated with economics, general management, strategy, the legal and social environment of business, organizational structure and dynamics, and business policy accounted for the remaining 40 percent.

Academic Jargon and Buzz Words

The list contains little jargon and few buzz words. Our large survey population decided, for example, that *power tie* is just too precious to be included on any index of literacy. *Power lunch,* on the other hand, got surprisingly favorable early reviews. But later interviews and surveys indicated that terms such as *power lunch* are not really central to the core of literacy. Some idioms, like *bottom line,* do contain a semantic richness and referential punch that gives them staying power. But usually these buzz words and phrases have no abiding content and, like all fashions, will probably not outlast their novelty. And so *power lunch* finally went the way of *executive washroom.* Here is a short sample of other terms that dropped off the list:

> *ASAP*
> *disintermediation*
> *FYI*
> *hygiene motivation (model)*
> *task significance*
> *boundary-spanning activities*

No Proper Names

There are no proper names on the list. To many, this may seem like a significant omission. Every manager, one could argue, probably should know the names of companies in the forefront of the news and the names of those managers and executives whose contributions to the business scene not only get them media attention but also give them a prominent place in the current life of the organizations they serve. The early list did not exclude these names. *McDonald's,* for example, was on the preliminary list because the name stands for more than itself: it represents worldwide franchising. The same could be said of Henry Ford and mass production, Adam Smith and the Invisible Hand, Alfred Sloan and decentralized organizations, and Steve Jobs and the personal computer. The question was, as always, where to draw the line. We left a lot of names on the preliminary list, but none of them received strong reviews. Indeed, we were surprised to see how unpopular proper names were with our survey populations.

Perhaps this unpopularity has something to do with the fact that celebrity, sensation, and fashion give many names a bright, but temporary, radiance. An implicit distinction, for example, between notoriety and importance resulted from all the surveys. Managers clearly did not want the list littered with here-today, gone-tomorrow celebrities and notables and seemed instead to recognize the importance of the concepts most closely associated with these figures. *Insider trading,* as mentioned previously, remained, and *Ivan Boesky* did not.

But every name from *Adam Smith* to *Lee Iacocca* fared poorly in the later survey ratings. We took this to mean that practicing managers were skeptical of the importance of merely knowing certain famous names. They seemed concerned not to let managerial literacy degenerate into name-dropping. We were relieved that the onus of a popularity contest would not be connected to the list. The poor ratings that names received certainly support the reputation of business as being largely impersonal. But managers were on the whole reasonably familiar with these names. For whatever reason, they were more apt to remember and accord importance to the ideas and activities associated with individuals than to the individuals themselves.

No Books

Not many managers found the titles of individual books to be important for their professional literacy, though the early list included works as diverse as *Das Kapital, The Wealth of Nations, The One-Minute Manager, The Art of Japanese Management, Getting to Yes,* and *Babbitt.* As with proper names, there seemed to be a general reluctance to include items that were only *associated* with business content and concerns, but had little such content in themselves. Another way of putting this is to say that titles were less important than were the ideas between the covers. Any literate manager should, of course, understand references to books by authors from Alexis de Tocqueville to Tom Peters, but this finally means less than understanding the basic concepts and arguments contained in these authors' works.

No Foreign Currencies

The early list contained several terms denoting foreign currencies *(pound, deutsche mark, yen, ruble),* but our survey populations rated them so poorly that we dropped them from the list. Most of these currencies, moreover, are so well known that any man or woman on the street would be likely to know them. It should be noted that the list also contains many financial terms that are known by different names in other countries. In England, for example, *accounts payable,* or *payables,* is equivalent to our *creditors;* and *earned surplus* is their term for our *retained earnings.*

Few Foreign Words

At one time, words such as *ringi* and *zaibatsu* were on the list, but, as was true of foreign currencies, managers did not consider them to be vital information. Unlike foreign currencies, many of which are commonly known by the average American, foreign words are not particularly well known, or they have an American English corollary that serves, however imperfectly, in their places. Such is the case, for instance, with the Japanese term *ringi,* which denotes a particular kind of decision-making process but has to a large extent been absorbed into our notion of participative management. In voting down many of the foreign terms on the survey list, managers might also be producing a kind of nationalistic mandate, a way of stating that the literacy of their business community is specifically American. Although the enterprises of multinational corporations are quickly literalizing the commonplace phrase *the world of business,* the list is preeminently an American one.

Durability

One sign of the relative stability of the business world (as reflected in its core language) is the fact that more than half the items on the literacy list are close to 20 years old. The so-called knowledge explosion has created a climate of near hysteria about all there is to know and the impossibility of keeping up. But the durability of the core knowledge that the list represents suggests that much recent innovation has been absorbed into an existing coherent managerial language. The new language is exciting, of course, and necessary if the business community is to keep pace with lasting changes. The managerial literacy list will doubtless need to be revised for the next century, but we predict that most of its elements will remain unchanged in the 1990s.

THE THRESHOLD OF LITERACY

The idea of literacy necessarily proposes a single threshold, or limit, above or below which managers could consider themselves either literate or illiterate. One CEO we interviewed suggested that the process of reaching the threshold of literacy was analogous to heating a block of ice until the solid turns liquid; at that point there is literally a "state change." This threshold cannot easily be pegged to a particular set of items since few managers will know all of the items and every manager will know a slightly different set. Knowing a high percentage of the items, of course, dramatically increases the chances of overlap with other managers. Likewise, as that percentage drops, the chances of *not* sharing important background knowledge with other managers (who also know only a percentage of the list) goes up exponentially.

To arrive at the final list, we cut 10 percent from the bottom of the survey list. If it were not for the convenient cutoff point suggested by the statistics, we could presumably have cut another 10 percent of the items from the list. Indeed, we might have kept cutting until we could say that all managers needed to know all the items. Instead, because we recognized that business activity is diverse and that not every manager needs to know every item, we have established that knowing 80 percent of the items on the list represents the minimum threshold of managerial literacy.

At percentages of 90 percent and above, for instance, it is very likely that two managers will not know two entirely different groups of 10 percent of the items. Two managers who each did not know a totally distinct 10 percent of the list would effectively share 80 percent of the information on it. But as the individual percentages decrease, so does the likelihood of there being no overlap in what they don't know. At 80 percent, in fact, it is as likely that the 20 percent of the items that the managers don't know will completely overlap as it is that they will not overlap at all. The manager who knows 80 percent of the items is likely to share a high percentage of these items with other literate managers.

The 80 percent threshold also made sense because the great bulk of the items that survived the final cut represented 80 percent of the survey list. It is possible, but not likely, for managers' gaps of 20 percent to fall entirely within a block of finance or accounting terms, for instance, or within any area in which they have had little contact or training. If, in going through the list, a manager finds that his or her gaps are concentrated in this way, it should be a simple matter to remedy the deficiency. It is far more likely, however, that these gaps will appear across the map of literacy. If that is the case, knowing only 80 percent—will be unlikely to cripple a manager.

If managers are not familiar with at least 80 percent of the terms, idioms, and concepts on the list, they radically diminish their ability to function effectively, flexibly, and responsibly. Ignorance of an entire functional area may not compromise a manager's career in the short run, but over the course of a career or given average ambitions, it can be dangerous to have such thin spots in one's literacy. By contrast, being familiar with at least 80 percent of the items on the literacy list ensures that one is generally acquainted with the basic vocabularies of all the major fields of business. Such a level of familiarity clearly responds to the need to stay globally competitive, professionally well rounded, and fortified against the many challenges of a full business career.

CHAPTER 3

IMPLICATIONS FOR MANAGERS

Identifying the core knowledge underlying the practice of management has been widely recognized as important in establishing management as a profession. Nevertheless, as Professor Ed Schein of MIT's Sloan School of Management asserted in a recent address to the Academy of Management, "There is no commonly agreed upon body of knowledge that is recognized as the essence of what is needed in order to be a manager."[1] Although some people have attempted to prescribe what managers presumably should know, even those well-meaning efforts have been formulated only in general terms.[2] By contrast, our managerial literacy list specifies what literate managers do know and find useful. It is the first systematic articulation of the actual knowledge used by successful managers in the practice of

---

[1] Edgar H. Schein, "Management Education: Some Troublesome Realities and Possible Remedies," *Journal of Management Development, 7,* no. 2 (March-April 1988), p. 9. His article is based on an original keynote address to the Management Education Division of the Academy of Management.

[2] American Assembly of Collegiate Schools of Business. *Accreditation Council, Policies, Procedures, and Standards.* (St. Louis: AACSB, 1986–1987). The American Assembly of Collegiate Schools of Business (AACSB) is the official accrediting agency for collegiate schools of business in the United States. The AACSB Curriculum Standards currently prescribe that member schools and candidates for accreditation "provide students with the common body of knowledge in business administration" by providing minimum course work in several areas of business. However, beyond broad descriptions of required course work, the "common body of knowledge" is not made explicit.

day-to-day management. As such, the list also represents the first comprehensive description of the language community of American business.

Those managers who know at least 80 percent of the items on the list—whether they manage small businesses or work in large multinational corporations—should feel confident that they can engage in meaningful conversations with other experienced managers. But the broad implications of this literacy and the knowledge it represents extend beyond this one-dimensional measurement. These implications may be grouped into three related categories. They are concerned with the individual manager's relation to this knowledge with the means to enhance the manager's own literacy, and with the challenge of providing opportunities for others to become more literate.

For individual managers, the literacy list offers a diagnostic standard by which to measure both the breadth and depth of their present knowledge. Such measurements allow managers to affirm their strengths and to put in high relief what they don't know. In coming to appreciate their current level of knowledge and to see what else there is to know, managers can begin to take charge of their professional development and careers. In times of unprecedented corporate restructuring, it is especially critical to maintain the flexibility that literacy provides.

The second set of implications clusters around the important relationship of managerial literacy to management education and development. Literacy develops through on-the-job work experience as well as through formal educational programs. By understanding the process through which one becomes managerially literate and the educational resources available to improve one's literacy, a manager can take charge of his or her own development. The core knowledge that the list represents also offers educators the chance to see how their programs are either in or out of step with what is currently thought and said in the business world. The list provides a way of assessing the needs of managers as they progress in their careers. Managerial literacy is by its very nature a call for lifelong learning, and the literacy list supplies both the context and the core content of a manager's education.

The third implication of this form of literacy concerns the responsibilities of managers and executives to provide for the ongoing growth and learning of the managers who work with them and for their organizations. For line managers, the list can provide important guidance in mentoring, in assessing their people's developmental needs over time, and in arranging for formal education and other broadening or deepening experiences. For human resource specialists, the list can suggest new ways of thinking about the role of corporate education programs in providing a managerially literate work force. For senior managers, ensuring a literate pool of managers for management succession has vital strategic implications; this task challenges them to provide the personal and institutional leadership necessary to create and sustain a corporate culture that promotes managerial literacy and lifelong learning.

UNDERSTANDING ONE'S LITERACY: IMPLICATIONS AND IMPORTANCE OF THE LIST

The idea of managerial literacy confronts managers with the importance of what they know and don't know about business. Working with the managerial literacy checklist in Chapter 4 makes explicit the idiosyncratic cache of business-related knowledge—from *accelerated depreciation* to *zero-based budgeting*—that individual practitioners have accumulated through professional experience and education.

Identifying the shape and boundaries of one's own literacy profile is an intriguing exercise. Almost all managers, for example, are familiar with terms such as *organization chart, board of directors, bottom line,* and *operating profit.* But beyond a core of a few hundred items known by all managers, the particular 80 percent known to a given literate manager is as unique as a fingerprint.

Those without the benefit of a formal education in management are often surprised and gratified to learn how much they know. For those with MBAs and/or other formal training in management, the list provides the opportunity to validate the contribution of their education to their literacy and to assess the cumulative impact of their subsequent work experience. Whether a manager has been trained at the Harvard Business School or the "school of hard knocks," a score of 80 percent or more on the list loudly proclaims the breadth and sufficiency of his or her knowledge and offers full membership in the language community of American management. For managers committed to continuing their professional development, the list provides a baseline against which to measure their growing literacy.

As managers work with the list and check off seemingly disparate terms such as *cash cow, marginal cost,* or *matrix organization,* the process brings into the foreground knowledge and associations they currently use as well as much of what they had forgotten they knew. The process challenges managers to "own" a vast set of ideas, concepts, and idioms that they had taken for granted. Until revealed through systematic inspection, a manager's literacy is as unapparent as is air to a bird or water to a fish.

The idea of managerial literacy as a largely invisible context that shapes the way managers think, communicate, and act is profoundly simple—*and* profoundly important. As asserted earlier, the process of management takes place largely through conversations with others inside and outside the organization. Reflecting on the knowledge that one shares in common with others in one's day-to-day organizational experience provides insight into the speed that shared knowledge adds to organizational communication.

Reflecting on one's own literacy profile—and the actual or imagined profiles of those with whom one works—also illuminates gaps between what some managers know and what others don't know. Seemingly intractable conflicts between groups or departments, inexplicable misunderstandings and personality conflicts, and generic communication problems can be powerfully reinterpreted by the thoughtful manager under the spotlight of managerial literacy. For example, the apparent indifference of a sales manager to corporate profitability may actually reflect a deficit in the cost-accounting dimensions of that manager's literacy. Similarly, the notion of different levels of literacy can allow a senior manager to understand why a newly articulated corporate strategy that inspires his own management team produces a lackluster response from middle managers or first-line supervisors.

The list also brings into sharp focus what managers themselves don't know. Experienced managers with careers in one function or specialized area of business may find that their knowledge is skewed. For example, a seasoned marketing manager in a large consumer-products company would undoubtedly know most or all of the marketing-oriented items on the list, terms such as *marketing mix, distribution channels, niche strategy, predatory pricing, segmentation, global branding,* and so on. And yet, if that manager's entire career had been in marketing, he or she would be predictably less conversant with terms familiar to most manufacturing managers such as *J-I-T, EOQ,* or *total quality management.*

Literacy suggests both an awareness of individual items and an understanding of a rich set of associations that underlies this knowledge. Managerial literacy thus represents a comprehensive map of a manager's knowledge—breadth *and* depth. *Breadth* refers to the range and reach of a manager's knowledge—the extent of one's working familiarity with words, concepts, and ideas from the broad range of functions and disciplines that underlie the list and the practice of management. *Depth* refers to one's understanding of the conceptual and practical force of the terms and concepts and to one's appreciation of the connectedness of much of the knowledge represented by the literacy list. Having depth essentially means being able to put a given term in a context that associates it with other terms that deepen its meaning or application. Because of its nature, the list reveals breadth more clearly than depth; this is because depth is hard to measure, varies with applications, and develops from breadth. Beyond the threshold level, however, breadth can serve as a proxy for depth—for appreciating all the conceptual nuances or practical applications of single terms.

Breadth is the basic staple for managers who want to be well rounded enough to move easily among the various fields of business or to attain general management positions. As organizations become increasingly complex and specialized, only broadly literate managers can provide an integrating perspective among diverse specialists. As Wally Stettinius, chairman of Cadmus Communications Corporation, observed in an interview:

> My sense is that nearly everyone in a key management position today manages people who know more about their specialties than he or she does. Therefore, managerial literacy would seem to be a critical enabling competency for general managers in helping them translate what the specialists are saying—for example, the lawyers, financial experts, marketing people, and information technologists—into a coherent strategy.[3]

Breadth and depth are both necessary in order to translate and integrate ideas of specialists effectively.

How one stacks up in breadth and depth is difficult to assess without an explicit standard, and the managerial literacy list provides such a benchmark. The list can confirm expected gaps in one's own knowledge, reveal blind spots, and serve to set in motion processes designed to improve one's literacy and to broaden one for positions of greater responsibility.

IMPROVING ONE'S LITERACY: THE DYNAMICS OF EXPERIENCE AND EDUCATION IN MANAGEMENT DEVELOPMENT

The managerial literacy list does not discriminate as to *how* a manager develops either breadth or depth. But most experienced managers know that on-the-job experience and some kind of education blend to form the kind of literacy that enhances a manager's effectiveness. Some managers argue that a lifetime of experience is the best school and that a manager's degree of

---

[3]Wallace Stettinius, in a conversation with the authors on February 28, 1989.

literacy directly correlates to the mass of business transactions with which a manager has been involved over the course of a career. Others assert that all the experience in the world is not sufficient to help a manager either to rise above what he or she already knows and can do well or to make a swift transition to another field. In such cases, education makes all the difference.

Consider how experience and education interact to produce breadth, depth, and various kinds and degrees of literacy and flexibility in a manager. Clearly a manager can know something conceptually without understanding it experientially, and vice versa. It is one thing to read about *Theory X* or *Theory Y*. It is another to encounter firsthand a *Theory X* superior. And it is quite another challenge, as a line manager, to attempt to live a *Theory Y* philosophy in daily practice. There are no clear routes to take in order to arrive at specific levels or depths of knowledge. How *much* a manager knows and how *well* a manager knows useful information can even work against one another. Textbook learning, for example, may give a manager exposure to a broad range of information but in insufficient depth to make it useful. Conversely, experience isn't always the best teacher because it can give managers exposure without deepening their conceptual understanding.

Ultimately, of course, how a manager comes by knowledge, assimilates it, and uses it are closely related. One experienced manager with whom we talked, Andy Crawford, focused these issues in a representative way. Despite the individual details of his business career, he speaks for thousands of experienced managers like him.

The Role of Hands-On Experience

Andy Crawford, a Florida businessman whose company has become one of the largest independent waste handlers in the state, started his business career after leaving the University of Florida in 1961, where he had studied industrial engineering. His first job was with Armstrong, but he left to join the Brunswick Corporation, following its acquisition of MacGregor, where he assisted in closing a manufacturing facility in Cincinnati and in relocating several new operations in the Southeast. In the late 1960s, Andy accepted a field-operations position with Farm Best Dairies, where he managed a six-state territory. Andy afterwards decided to return to Florida, and he accepted a corporate staff position with Industrial America, a $60-million conglomerate with interests in manufacturing, real estate, and distribution. With the company headed for bankruptcy, Andy later resigned to become a regional manager for Waste Resources Corporation. In 1977 Andy switched his career path and founded Southland Waste Systems, which he built into a successful $10-million business.

Andy knew most of the items on the list, but he suggested that many managers probably would not have reached his literacy level:

> I think it would be unusual to find any young manager who would be familiar with a high percentage of the words you have here. It's not just a lack of education, however, but also a lack of having lived it through their experience in the business world. The problem would be that they would not yet have had the experiences necessary in order to understand these words and terms in the business world.

Andy emphasized that his familiarity with the principles and terms on the list was largely a function of his broad experience. They were terms that he'd run into over a diverse business career. Moreover, the idea of managerial literacy helped him to understand the components of his experience and articulate the reasons for his successes.

> For example, you have *balance sheet, bankruptcy, cash flow,* and *cash management.* I sure lived through a lot of these terms during the plant closings at Brunswick and in my management experiences during the failure of the conglomerate. I learned how to read a balance sheet, which I can do about as well as my controller. And I learned to understand cash flow and the difference between cash flow, profit, and cash management.
>
> It's a different world when you're a small business. And many of these terms on the list are things which I understand and which I think many managers don't. Again, take *cash manage-*

ment, cash flow, and *profit.* There's a time when you need an emphasis on the balance sheet, and there's a time when you need an emphasis on cash. It's critical that managers understand what their goals are, and that those change depending on the kind of environment that they're in and on what they're trying to accomplish.

In a small business like mine, in order to grow as fast as I have and do as well as I have done, you have to be able to understand *leverage ratios*—and a lot of other terms on the list. My debt-to-equity is about three-to-one, and it's comfortable because of the fact that I manage my cash flow and understand what it takes to service the debt while growing at the rate I want to grow. I think that if I hadn't had the background in management and the experience with most of the words on this list before I went into my own business, it could have been a disaster.

In discussing the relationship between cash flow, profit, and cash management, Andy displayed a rare depth. He realized that he began to mature as a manager only after he started his own business. Before that, his ability to rely on corporate staffs insulated him from understanding the deeper connections and from applying the kind of knowledge he had picked up. As an entrepreneur, he was forced to take a lot of the terms and put them to work. Andy's managerial trajectory may not represent the typical corporate career path, but his exposure to a wide range of businesses and functions clearly provided him with a degree of literacy he didn't know he had:

I have no doubt that the sum total of all the things I've done in my business life—the things that worked and the things that didn't work—have contributed to me as a manager. It's given me a certain seasoning—the sum total of all one's screw-ups and successes—such that, when faced with a problem or a new situation, I'm able to make quality decisions. I think that one of the ingredients that young managers lack is having been seasoned through experience. However capable and highly educated they are, it's an ongoing, day-to-day challenge to have them hammer out the issues the way an experienced manager would—and to come in with solutions.

Even though Andy had reason to prize the value of his experience, he also recognized the role of formal education in developing managerial literacy:

If I had it to do all over again and hadn't been burned out on school, I would have opted to finish my industrial engineering degree at Gainesville and gone on to get an MBA. In my opinion, I think that anybody that wants to pursue business as a career ought to get an MBA.

Andy's strong suit was his exposure to many facets of business life; and the breadth and depth of his experiences—both his misfortunes and triumphs—seasoned him. His example represents one way of becoming managerially literate, and it illustrates the virtues of experience over theory in the depth that can develop without formal education. While thousands of managers grow into literacy in roughly the same way Andy did, many others become managerially literate through more formal means.

The Role of Formal Learning

Beyond learning from experience, one can obviously acquire facility with the concepts and terms on the literacy list through some kind of formal learning. (*Formal learning,* as used here, means that the acquisition of knowledge occurs other than through work experience and away from one's immediate job.) Many terms and idioms have a richness that can't be grasped through hands-on experience, and formal learning can provide an understanding of abstract principles that underpin them and give them conceptual force and depth.

Managers committed to honing their own managerial literacy—and the literacy of those for whom they are responsible—can avail themselves of a number of resources, including self-instruction programs, books, and business periodicals. However, the most important resources for becoming fully literate are undergraduate and graduate schools of business and corporate management-education and -training programs.

The Business Schools
For many American managers and managers-to-be, the development of managerial literacy begins in college. Indeed, in the

1990s Americans are attending college and university programs in business and management in record numbers:

- Of the 12 million Americans currently enrolled in institutions of higher learning, over one million are enrolled in undergraduate business and management programs,[4] and over 220,000 are enrolled in graduate programs.[5]
- Some 1,500 American schools offer associate or undergraduate degrees in business and management, and over 600 offer graduate degrees.[6]
- Approximately one third of the undergraduates and approximately two thirds of those working on graduate degrees attend part-time.[7]
- 75,000 new MBAs are entering the work force annually, a threefold increase in two decades.[8]

For those committed to expanding their literacy, America's business schools represent a great resource. However, as Professors Lyman Porter and Lawrence McKibbin point out in *Management Education: Drift or Thrust into the 21st Century?*, a recent, comprehensive, multiyear study:

> In today's world, and most definitely in the world of tomorrow, a person's management education cannot stop with the completion of a formal bachelor's or master's degree program in business or any other relevant subject. If it did, such an individual would rapidly become relegated to the "also rans" rather than continuing to be a member of that group expected to provide leadership—at whatever organizational level—in the management sectors of our society's institutions.[9]

Unfortunately, Porter and McKibbin found little evidence of any systematic planning and attention by business or management

---

[4]*1988 Digest of Educational Statistics* (Washington, D.C.: National Center for Education Statistics, 1988), p. 144.

[5]Eugene Miller, *Barron's Guide to Graduate Business Schools* (New York: Barron's, 1988), Preface.

[6]*1988 Digest of Educational Statistics*, p. 214.

[7]*1988 Digest of Educational Statistics*, p. 163.

[8]*1988 Digest of Educational Statistics*, p. 163.

[9]Lyman W. Porter and Lawrence E. McKibbin, *Management Education and Development: Drift or Thrust into the 21st Century?* (New York: McGraw-Hill, 1988), p. 217.

schools about meeting the needs of managers and corporations for lifelong learning. Rather, with respect to these needs, they report that "the most descriptive operative word . . . in business schools has been *complacency.*"[10] Fortunately, for the working manager with a company tuition-reimbursement plan, the managerial literacy list can provide an important resource in planning educational experiences that provide an appropriate counterpart to work experience.

Corporate Management Development

In addition to tuition-reimbursement plans for the programs of colleges and universities, nearly all large companies have formal management-development programs today. Indeed, the investment by American companies is staggering:

- According to a Carnegie Foundation report, corporations spend $40 to $60 billion annually in providing formal educational experiences for nearly eight million employees;[11] another report estimates that American companies spend an additional $180 billion annually in unstructured on-the-job training.[12]
- A survey of the largest industrial and service corporations in America reported that 60 companies (including IBM, Xerox, Kodak, Burroughs, AT&T, New England Telephone, CIGNA, and Nationwide Insurance) owned corporate education centers, some with curricula and facilities rivaling college programs.[13]
- To broaden executives beyond their specialized or limited careers, corporations are currently sending more than 15,000 executives annually to residential university management programs at over 50 universities in the United States and Canada.[14]

---

[10] Porter and McKibbin, *Management Education and Development,* pp. 310–11.

[11] N. Eurich, *Corporate Classrooms* (Princeton: Carnegie Foundation for the Advancement of Teaching), 1985, p. 5.

[12] *The Wall Street Journal,* August 5, 1986.

[13] Walter A. Green and Harold Lazarus, "Corporate Campuses: A Growing Phenomenon," *Journal of Management Development,* 7, no. 3 (May-June 1988).

[14] Chistopher Billy, ed., *1989 Bricker's International Directory: University Executive Programs,* (Princeton: Peterson's Guides, 1989), p. v.

- Taken as a whole, enrollments in corporate education programs and expenditures by corporations in educating their employees are approaching the total annual expenditures and enrollments of all the nation's four-year colleges and graduate schools.[15]

For managers committed to expanding their literacy, this investment may provide a great opportunity. Nevertheless, in a survey of 249 corporate heads of management development, some 41 percent indicated that the typical manager in their companies spends two or fewer workdays per year attending formal management-development programs, and only 10 percent stated that each manager in their organizations was required to attend such programs.[16]

Part of the problem is an absence of management commitment. Consider the findings, for instance, of a recent comprehensive study of the effectiveness of corporate education that was conducted by the Columbia University Graduate School of Business under the sponsorship of Allied-Signal, Inc.[17] After interviews with senior human resource executives from America's leading corporations, the research team surveyed heads of corporate education from 250 companies selected from *Fortune* magazine's list of "America's Most Admired Corporations" and conducted follow-up interviews with a number of the respondents. The researchers found that, while 90 percent of the respondents believed their companies *should* be highly committed to both formal learning experiences and career planning for middle managers and executives, only 40 percent reported that such practices were actually followed! Also, the study reported that programs for education and programs for career planning were typically conducted with relative independence rather than being linked. In such companies, managers presumably see no relationship between educating themselves and their opportunities for promotions or advancement.

---

[15]Robert M. Fulmer, "Corporate Management Development: The State of the Art," *Journal of Management Development,* 7, no. 2, (March-April 1988), p. 57.

[16] Porter and McKibbin, *Management Education and Development* p. 254.

[17]Fulmer, "Corporate Management Development."

Those who are ambitious and responsible about their future must find ways to continue learning on their own. The managerial literacy list, used in consultation with one's boss and corporate education specialists, provides the proactive manager with a basis for taking charge of the development of his or her own literacy.

Ensuring one's own literacy is especially critical in a period of almost unprecedented organizational restructuring. Consider the impact on American managers of the fact that during the past 10 years U.S. companies have participated in nearly 24,000 mergers and acquisitions.[18] The annual dollar value of these business transactions approached $200 billion[19], and it has been estimated that 10 percent of the U.S work force—nearly 12 million people—has been influenced by these transformations.[20] Whether caught in a merger, leveraged buyout, acquisition, divestiture, or planned downsizing, middle managers and older senior managers have been particularly vulnerable to being outplaced. According to one source, over a million managers lost their jobs during the 1980s; tens of thousands of additional managers have had their roles redefined and/or been relocated as a result of organizational restructuring.[21] Most of the managers affected had done nothing to prepare themselves for alternative jobs or new careers, nor had their bosses encouraged or sponsored such preparation. This statistic provides a powerful stimulus for using managerial literacy and the list in a fresh way to plan one's own development and expand one's career options.

---

[18]Janet L. Neiman, ed., *Mergerstat Review—1987* (Chicago: W. T. Grimm and Company, 1988). Data are for the 10-year period 1978–87.

[19]*1988 Statistical Abstract of the United States* (Washington, D.C.: U.S. Department of Commerce, 1988), p. 504. According to "Mergers and Acquisitions: Historical Summary," one section of this abstract, there were 3,336 net mergers and acquisitions in 1986, with a dollar value paid of $173.1 billion.

[20]Anthony F. Buono and James L. Bowditch, *The Human Side of Mergers and Acquisitions: Managing Collisions between People, Cultures and Organizations* (San Francisco: Jossey-Bass, 1989), p. 5.

[21]Buono and Bowditch, *The Human Side of Mergers and Acquisitions,* p. 5.

ENHANCING OTHERS' LITERACY: ORGANIZATIONAL RESPONSIBILITY

Beyond the responsibility of the individual for managing his or her own development, managers and executives at every level of an organization are responsible for creating a climate in which learning is valued and people are encouraged to enrich, broaden, and deepen their literacy. The managerial literacy list can be an invaluable tool in meeting this responsibility.

For example, line managers can use the list to identify areas of their own knowledge and understanding that they can contribute to their employees through on-the-job coaching or other informal training activities. They can use gaps identified in employees as a basis for working with these employees to develop and implement plans to round out their literacy through job rotation, career planning, employee participation in college or company-based educational experiences, and other developmental experiences.

Management educators and corporate education staffs can use the managerial literacy list to ensure that managers do not become obsolete. Even individuals with MBAs or other degrees in business or management can become disenfranchised if they do not continue to add relevant new knowledge, renew and deepen the knowledge and skills they learned in school, and find new ways to apply that knowledge.

The managerial literacy list can also be used for purposes of ongoing organizational diagnosis and research similar to the research done in developing the list. Management educators can then move quickly to provide forward-thinking programs to ensure that the organization as a whole achieves sufficient literacy to allow it to function effectively. The list can thus provide a fresh perspective on ways in which corporate education programs can complement the learning of degreed entry-level managers.

Top managements need to sponsor educational programs that help create a corporate culture in which managers at various levels and in different departments are able to communicate with the ease that managerial literacy allows. The President and CEO of Pizza Hut, Inc., Steve Reinemund, offered several examples in which his organization tried to bring talented operations people from the field into the home office:

> They couldn't survive against the MBAs, so we sent them back to school. It was extremely satisfying when they subsequently became thought leaders.[22]

Reinemund and other enlightened senior executives recognize the need to provide for the continuous development of general management perspectives throughout their companies and to ensure the maintenance of a pool of literate managers for senior-management succession. They must make public the view that the development and maintenance of literacy is an *investment* in the managerial vitality of their company—not a cost. They need to demand that systems be developed that link education with career enhancement. And in a time of mergers, acquisitions, LBOs, and divestitures, they need to provide for the broad-based literacy that will create flexibility for individual managers—and for the organization—as managerial resources must be redeployed.

One of the cases in our research poignantly demonstrates the human and organizational costs of failing in this effort to ensure the development of appropriate managerial literacy. It is a real story, based on an all-too-familiar series of individual and organizational mishaps and misjudgments, of how *not* to succeed in business, try as one might.

The case involves a manager who genuinely tried to grow with his job but who consistently found himself thwarted by the new exigencies and challenges of his career. Although he is partly responsible for not recognizing his own ignorance—that is, not knowing how much he didn't know—he is no more to blame than is the organization that failed to provide him with the guidance necessary to allow him to develop an adequate literacy.

---

[22]Steve Reinemund, in a telephone interview with the authors on May 4, 1989.

The Case of John P. Finch

John P. Finch graduated from a well-known midwestern university with a bachelor's degree in computer science. Following graduation, he accepted a job in his home town with "AmerCo," an internationally known consumer-products company, as a programmer in the department of information systems. The department was responsible for developing large computer-based systems for the firm's global operations.

John's first assignment was to write computer code for the intelligent workstation front end of a global electronic mail system. Unfortunately, John hadn't learned the appropriate programming language at his university. So he took a course through AmerCo's professional education department. After a few months, he was quite proficient and was programming successfully, using specification documents provided by the system's designers.

After a series of positive annual performance appraisals, and given his persistent expression of interest in moving into a management track, John was promoted to project leader in systems development, where he was responsible for a group of five programmers and systems analysts. In the early stages of his first assignment, creating a large billing system, John was asked by his manager to attend a meeting with the group's internal clients, who were middle-management representatives from the firm's operating divisions. John's charge was to create the specification document that would outline the clients' needs. During the meeting, the clients talked rapidly about their requirements, using terms like *accounts receivable, discounts and allowances, arrearage, cash basis, general ledger, cash management, cost centers, delay allowance, EOQ, fiscal year,* and *item cost.* John was somewhat confused by the conversation, but he didn't want to admit his ignorance or slow the meeting down, so he rapidly took notes.

About a week after the meeting, recognizing that he and his team lacked expertise in accounting, John asked his manager for permission to take a company-sponsored course in basic accounting. But his boss said that he was under too much time pressure to give John time off. "We've got to get this system out!" he said. Meanwhile, John and his systems-development professionals, none of whom knew very much about business, worked on the specification document that presumably defined what the clients needed. Six months later, in a review meeting, the client managers rejected the specification document as reflecting "little real understanding of our business."

Because of his natural ability with people and the shortage of qualified managers for systems-development positions, John was promoted to manager of office automation systems. He was pleased to get the promotion into a management job because, by then, new technologies had largely displaced programmers with the skills that he had. The new job appealed to him, except for his frustration with the time-consuming management reports. Shortly after his promotion, he attended a course for new managers, "Interpersonal Skills for New Managers," at the request of the human resources department.

His new position included the maintenance of the electronic mail system for which he had helped write computer code five years previously. In reviewing it, John was shocked to find that the system, which had taken three years and millions of dollars to develop, wasn't being used. He wondered if there was anything to learn from the billing-system project.

After several frustrating years of trying to deal with the formidable pace of technological change and with escalating development costs and demands of users, John wanted to transfer out of the systems department. The only opportunities, however, were in the product marketing area, and John lacked any relevant knowledge or experience. To demonstrate his good intentions, though, and to learn something about marketing, he enrolled in a night course in marketing at a local college. AmerCo paid the tuition. Unfortunately, before he was able to convince the company that he was a suitable candidate for a position in marketing, John's position and entire department were eliminated. The cut occurred as a result of a restructuring precipitated by the takeover of AmerCo by "SwissCo," a European multinational, and by SwissCo's decision to centralize and standardize systems throughout the company.

John was subsequently offered a job in the corporate systems department at SwissCo's North American headquarters in Los Angeles. With mixed feelings, he declined because he wanted to broaden his management expertise beyond systems-development work. He and his wife were also reluctant to raise their young children in southern California and to confront the lifestyle changes that the cost of housing there might require.

John considered going to school full-time to get an MBA, but that plan was not financially feasible. He took a temporary job to make ends meet and dropped his night course to devote evenings to his job search. After six months, John was still looking for the right job. The only major prospect seemed to be a position as a program-maintenance manager in a municipal government office, which he declined on the grounds that he wanted to get out of systems. He and his family managed to get by on the salary of John's wife, who had been able to create a half-time position that she job-shared with another mother.

John Finch didn't have Andy Crawford's opportunities to build breadth. His managerial illiteracy clearly undermined his effectiveness in developing user-oriented systems. He quickly became a victim of his illiteracy and of a management-development program that failed to help him plan for his or his corporation's future. The accounting courses offered through the corporate education program might have helped, but even the night course that he took in marketing was too little, too late to prepare him for other career choices.

The cost to John Finch was enormous, and the cost to the corporation was equally large. The courses in accounting that John's manager asserted John "didn't have time for" cost the organization two person-years of development time— approximately $150,000. Add to this figure an estimated $375,000 that can be attributed to a delay of at least six months in a system designed to produce an annual payback of $750,000 in reduced accounts receivable. Given the cost of developing a poorly conceived system or delaying its delivery by months or years, the lack of systematic management education for the AmerCo programmers and analysts involved in developing management systems seems terribly short-sighted.

John made the decision to move into management early in his technical career. If he had been conversant with the list and the underlying notions of managerial literacy, he would have seen clearly how much he didn't know and could have sought counsel with his boss or with the corporate education department. His boss obviously should have been much more active in helping John identify gaps between what he knew and what he needed to know to design effective systems and to enhance his future managerial flexibility. With John's permission, and using literacy and the list as a basis for discussion, he could have worked with John to develop and implement a long-term development plan consistent with John's vision for his career at AmerCo. Such a plan might have included mentoring and sharing his own business knowledge, encouraging John to visit client offices informally, arranging for job rotation or other broadening experiences outside of the systems-development department, and appropriate corporate and university-based courses in management.

The human resources and corporate education departments at AmerCo must also bear some responsibility. After all, managerial literacy is no more amenable to a quick fix than is the development of competence in computer systems design. Those responsible for education departments need to understand that an occasional course in human relations or accounting won't turn a systems analyst into a literate manager.

The Role of Management

The development and maintenance of managerial literacy requires individual initiative, systematic corporate education programs linked to career development, and active support for lifelong learning that begins with top management and is demonstrated at every management level of the organization. Stan Davis, author and noted management consultant, reports that he once asked a senior executive responsible for the future development of a very large corporation what he worried most about. The executive's answer was provocative and relevant:

> I worry most about what my people don't know that they don't know. What they know that they don't know, they are able to work on and find the answers to. But they can't do that if they don't know what they don't know.[23]

With respect to managerial literacy, this statement is at the heart of the matter for top management. After all, it is ultimately the top management of a company that is accountable for what their managers "don't know that they don't know." It is the top management that is accountable for the consequences of organizational illiteracy and blind spots and that must provide leadership to create a climate and corporate culture that encourages, supports, and reinforces widespread literacy and lifelong learning for all employees.

Some organizations and their top managements are obviously more vigilant than others when it comes to keeping managers sufficiently educated. Stew Leonard's, the "world's largest dairy store" in Norwalk, Connecticut, is an example of an organization that nurtures its managers by paying attention to their lifelong learning needs. The business is cited as an exemplar of effective management in the book *A Passion for Excellence*[24] and was the subject of a popular public television special on excellent companies, a show that included Disney World, IBM, Apple Computer, and the 3M Company.[25] Founded as a family business in 1916, Stew Leonard's employs over 700 people, enjoys annual revenues approaching $100 million in a single location, and manages to record sales per square foot of nearly ten times the industry average.[26]

---

[23]Stanley M. Davis, "Transforming Organizations: The Key to Strategy Is Context," *Organizational Dynamics,* Winter 1982, p. 64.

[24]Tom Peters and Nancy Austin, *A Passion for Excellence: The Leadership Difference,* (Warner Books: New York, 1986), p. 129.

[25]Sam Tyler and John Nathan, "In Search of Excellence," Public Broadcasting System, 1985.

[26]Peters and Austin, *A Passion for Excellence,* p. 66. At the time of the interview, Stew Leonard's was also operating a tent store in Danbury, Connecticut.

Stew Leonard, Jr., the president of Stew Leonard's, has an MBA from UCLA, years of experience "working the store," and a unique perspective on the interplay between hands-on experience and formal education in the development of managerial literacy. Stew has a deep respect for learning on the job and sees his father and Frank Perdue of Perdue Farms as examples of managers who learned about business in the school of hard knocks: "They don't have a lot of fancy education," said Stew in an interview, "but they are very sharp guys—*managerially literate*, to use your term—and really understand things like production management."[27] Indeed, Perdue has built a billion-dollar-a-year business in selling a commodity—chickens—at margins that reportedly reach seven to eight times the industry average and achieve market shares above 50 percent in major markets.[28] Stew Leonard's is Frank Perdue's largest single-store buyer. Despite the successes of his role models, Leonard recognizes the limitations of on-the-job experience for those less seasoned than Frank Perdue or his father:

> The people who come up through the ranks are really well grounded as far as handling the customer and can call good shots from their gut. But those people who haven't really learned about personnel management, about production management, who haven't learned about finance, don't see the whole realm of the problem the way a managerially literate person would. For us to keep growing, we need to provide ongoing education for our people, because our business is getting far more complex. If our people were managerially literate, the business would be managed better. We would have happier customers.
>
> On Sunday mornings, we're real busy, and rather than have a bunch of notes in the suggestion box saying, "I didn't see any meat out here until 8:00 in the morning," I'd rather have a manager who studied our hourly customer counts and then scheduled his production accordingly. Right now we're putting out so much product that we have to have people who know how to do production schedules instead of just coming in and saying, "I'll just cut around 10,000 pounds of chopped chuck." They have

---

[27]Stew Leonard, in a conversation with Jack Weber in Toronto, April 21, 1989.
[28]Peters and Austin, *A Passion for Excellence*, p. 66.

to know how much to grind in advance. Education makes you think ahead. It lets you know why there is a problem and what the possible solutions are.

Stew Leonard believes that a person in his organization who was formally and rigorously trained in forecasting and planning production lot sizes, for example, can see new possibilities for managing that others can't see. Stew spoke to the need for providing greater depth for managers at all levels of an organization in courses that are relevant to their functional specialization. But he acknowledged that managers also need broadening in ways that they can not always anticipate. That is the reason senior-management commitment to expanding the literacy of managers is so important; otherwise, he said, "The competition will just rip you to shreds and gobble you up!" That commitment is critical, regardless of the size and type of organization.

Senior managers and management-development specialists of large corporations must be as attentive to the educational needs of the people in the organizations as Stew Leonard is. He knows that good managers take charge of their own professional development and continuing education and that the role of a general manager is to be responsive to employees' ambitions by offering the proper programs at the right time so that no employee ends up like John Finch. Being a capable, caring general manager also means being a student, a teacher, and a leader.

LITERACY AND LEADERSHIP

The popular media, the business press, and the American academic community have recently aligned themselves in their search for a deeper understanding of the decline in American competitive preeminence. This commitment to new perspectives on management promises to help revitalize American enterprise and to prepare managers to deal with an increasingly complex, competitive, and fast-changing world. This discussion of managerial literacy springs from the same type of commitment and is designed to provoke a fundamental rethinking of the roots of managerial expertise and to stimulate much-needed research and improvement in management education.

Some of this rethinking is already taking place. In a recent article in *The Economist,* for instance, Tom Peters, the well-known management consultant and critic, urged sweeping changes in management education:

> Today's management wisdom is predicated on stability. None of its tools—basic accounting practices, patterns of organization, formulation of strategy or workforce care—can cope with the new rates of change.[29]

Peters's stirring call for revolutionary thinking in a world of discontinuous change is welcome, but in his zeal he overlooks something important in how managers will cope with such changes. Managers will still have to *manage* in these shifting environments, and they will still have to understand the direction of the executives whose responsibility it is to lead them in the future. Leaders, too, will have to understand the logic, the limits, and the potential of the managerial community on which they depend. It is in this context that managerial literacy gains importance as a means to bring new ideas and changing values into focus, not to enforce conformity to outdated tools and practices.

As a broad-based foundation of basic knowledge, managerial literacy makes it possible for one to cope with bewildering alterations without sacrificing one's capacity to see just how much useful knowledge endures through all the changes. Stan Davis, in his recent book, *Future Perfect,* puts it this way:

> When dealing with the fundamental transformation of an economy, it is essential to grasp the abstractions on which it is premised. However removed these may appear to be, ultimately they derive from our understanding of the fundamentals.[30]

---

[29]Tom Peters, "Tomorrow's Companies: New Products, New Markets, New Competition, New Thinking," *The Economist,* March 4, 1989, pp. 19–22.
[30]Stanley M. Davis, *Future Perfect* (Reading, Mass.: Addison-Wesley, 1987), p. 187.

This book on managerial literacy can be seen as offering a kind of present-perfect sense of the fundamentals without which one cannot even hope to grasp the abstractions that will generate economic change. Being managerially literate basically means feeling comfortable using vocabularies from all the major fields of business; it also means one can begin to grasp, and perhaps alter, the larger patterns of business practice. Managers can become leaders. While getting back to basics is the first best aim and virtue of managerial literacy, the list is not merely a set of inert facts to be assimilated and manipulated. It is also a challenge to general managers and senior executives to take a hard look at how disparate literacy levels may be inhibiting communications in their corporations or preventing certain middle-level managers from performing as well as they might in their jobs.

For senior managers and CEOs, managerial literacy is an invitation to think in fresh and insightful ways about their responsibility to the members of their organizations. Leaders must avail themselves of the possibilities of literacy if they are to create the context for lifelong learning. Executives must realize that they can directly affect both the breadth and depth of knowledge of the managers in their businesses, small or large. The idea of managerial literacy and the managerial literacy list can be used to create powerful new educational ventures and to establish new partnerships between individual managers and their organizations. And for those who wish to lead as well as manage, managerial literacy can supply a context in which to envision a future for business that business has not yet imagined for itself.

CHAPTER 4

THE MANAGERIAL
LITERACY LIST

The managerial literacy list presented in this chapter repre-sents the current benchmark of the language that managers use to talk to one another and to function effectively in the work-place. There are 1,200 items on the list. The number is arbitrary, in the sense that we had no predetermined limit on the size of the final list. We arrived at the final number naturally, by explaining the dimensions of literacy and then asking managers and executives to exclude unimportant items and add other, important ones. We believe that the list is reasonably complete and current, but we welcome your suggestions for further inclusions, and we invite your views about what ought not to remain on the list.[1]

Individual readers will certainly see specific items as more or less central to their experience and their jobs. Nevertheless, a literate manager should know at least 80 percent of the items on this list. Knowing less than that poses a challenge to one's professional development. In the absence of this knowledge, a range of references, and the associations and actions tied to them, will be lost. Some of those references and associations may never crop up in the daily conversations and transactions of your business. If you know only 75 percent of the items, you are not

---

[1]Please send any correspondence to the Foundation for Managerial Literacy, P.O. Box 1836, Williamsburg, Virginia, 23185.

necessarily illiterate. But you will undoubtedly benefit from knowing the remaining 25 percent.

This list has been designed as a checklist to make it easier to assess what you know and don't know. The entries have been randomized so that readers can examine and weigh each item individually. If you want to cross-check a given item or set of items, you can look up the item in Appendix following, which provides an alphabetized list and includes the provenance for each item on the list.

THE MANAGERIAL LITERACY LIST: A CHECKLIST

_____ acquisition

_____ restructuring

_____ balance sheet

_____ debt

_____ floating capacity

_____ fixed exchange rate

_____ Fortress Europe

_____ UAW

_____ Ma Bell

_____ disinflation

_____ savings

_____ cost classification

_____ gold standard

_____ FDIC

_____ product line

Page Total _____

_____ top management

_____ notes payable (and receivable)

_____ product substitution

_____ equity capital

_____ payroll

_____ merchandising

_____ standard data

_____ telemarketing

_____ achievement motivation

_____ program trading

_____ discounted cash flow

_____ money supply

_____ P/E ratio

_____ exponential smoothing

_____ self-actualization

_____ owners' equity

_____ projected cost

_____ cost behavior

_____ markup

_____ nominal GNP

_____ intrinsic reward

_____ Sherman Antitrust Act

_____ business-as-usual

_____ marginal analysis

_____ loading

_____ trade surplus (or deficit)

_____ J-I-T (just-in-time)

Page Total   _____

_____ mode

_____ brand management

_____ straight-line depreciation

_____ blacklisting

_____ sequential sampling

_____ base year

_____ GATT (General Agreement on Tariffs and Trade)

_____ monetary base

_____ service economy

_____ termination

_____ code of ethics

_____ natural monopoly

_____ programming language

_____ monetary policy

_____ accounting entity concept

_____ protectionism

_____ days' sales in accounts receivable

_____ conflict management

_____ slush fund

_____ Robinson-Patman Act of 1936

_____ separable cost

_____ team building

_____ Dow Jones Industrial Average (the Dow)

_____ operational budgeting

_____ PERT (program evaluation and review technique)

_____ private placement

_____ intensive distribution

Page Total _____

_____ hostile takeover

_____ time-series analysis

_____ business strategy

_____ flow chart

_____ uncollectible account

_____ workstation

_____ sunset provision

_____ capital formation

_____ subcontracting

_____ letter of credit

_____ job enrichment

_____ stockout cost

_____ Phillips curve

_____ depletion allowance

_____ management audit

_____ equity

_____ market follower

_____ dependent demand

_____ net worth

_____ capital budgeting

_____ the Fed (Federal Reserve System)

_____ promotional pricing

_____ specialization of labor

_____ golden handcuffs

_____ potential GNP

_____ competitive advantage

_____ relevant inventory cost

Page Total _____

_____ trial balance

_____ responsibility accounting

_____ greenmail

_____ profit center

_____ precontract planning

_____ attrition rate

_____ monetary indicator

_____ market order

_____ debt/equity ratio

_____ poison pill

_____ antitrust legislation

_____ intergroup conflict

_____ target market

_____ derived demand

_____ type A

_____ HRM (human resource management)

_____ return on incremental investment

_____ practical capacity

_____ selective perception

_____ strike price

_____ money center bank

_____ underground economy

_____ voice mail

_____ prisoner's dilemma

_____ zero defects

_____ median

_____ sustainable growth

Page Total _____

_____ downsizing

_____ inventory

_____ money manager

_____ start date

_____ state unemployment compensation tax

_____ national debt

_____ jobber

_____ book value

_____ resource allocation

_____ MITI

_____ cost

_____ mass market

_____ Gresham's Law

_____ promissory note

_____ FICA

_____ disequilibrium

_____ skim pricing

_____ CPA

_____ corporate strategy

_____ credit

_____ continuous improvement

_____ vertical integration

_____ velocity of money

_____ listed stock

_____ withholding tax

_____ minimum rate of return

_____ purchasing power

Page Total _____

_____ judgmental forecasting

_____ subsidy

_____ consumer benefit

_____ EEC (European Economic Community)

_____ job rotation

_____ mean time between failures

_____ cartel

_____ strong dollar

_____ interlocking directorates

_____ divisional structure

_____ fixed manufacturing overhead

_____ MLP (master limited partnership)

_____ repurchase agreement (repo)

_____ incremental cost

_____ LIFO (last-in, first-out)

_____ goodwill

_____ market demand

_____ perfect (and imperfect) competition

_____ IMF (International Monetary Fund)

_____ P&L (profit and loss)

_____ depreciation

_____ cost of capital

_____ couponing

_____ allocated cost

_____ management team

_____ tie-in promotion

_____ flat organization

Page Total _____

_____ cost-profit-volume analysis

_____ fiscal policy

_____ Peter Principle

_____ disposable income

_____ accrued revenue

_____ law of supply and demand

_____ market penetration

_____ division of labor

_____ serial bonds

_____ postpurchase behavior

_____ CBOE (Chicago Board Options Exchange)

_____ real GNP

_____ stock split

_____ classical economics

_____ manufacturer's rep

_____ autocrat

_____ franchise

_____ type I error

_____ single proprietorship

_____ optional feature pricing

_____ middle management

_____ electronic mail (E-mail)

_____ corrective action

_____ hyperinflation

_____ latent market

_____ internal marketing

_____ role conflict

Page Total   _____

_____ work-in-process inventory

_____ weighted average cost of capital

_____ American Stock Exchange (AMEX)

_____ Reaganomics

_____ LAN (local area network)

_____ CRP (capacity requirements planning)

_____ business cycle

_____ ledger account

_____ sealed bid pricing

_____ linear regression

_____ hurdle rate

_____ industrial policy

_____ random number

_____ consumer protection

_____ regressive tax

_____ syndication

_____ job satisfaction

_____ quantity discount

_____ swap

_____ historical cost

_____ group process

_____ Invisible Hand

_____ specialty goods

_____ price cuts

_____ consumerism

_____ hands-on manager

_____ spinoff

Page Total _____

_____ organizational structure

_____ IRS (Internal Revenue Service)

_____ depression

_____ position power

_____ transfer pricing

_____ bond

_____ VAT (value added tax)

_____ objective function

_____ leverage ratios

_____ present value

_____ structural unemployment

_____ stock average

_____ deficit spending

_____ shark repellent

_____ bargaining unit

_____ brainstorming session

_____ investment tax credit

_____ currency appreciation (and depreciation)

_____ prospectus

_____ liabilities

_____ core business

_____ yield rate on bonds

_____ audit committee

_____ amortization

_____ job security

_____ EBIT (earnings before income tax)

_____ residual value

_____ 80–20 Rule

Page Total _____

_____ market growth rate

_____ stock option

_____ continuous production

_____ trade discount

_____ distributed data processing

_____ debit

_____ partial sampling

_____ regression analysis

_____ laissez-faire

_____ Theory _Z_

_____ Fed wire

_____ global market

_____ T-bill (treasury bill)

_____ CFO

_____ database

_____ Subchapter S corporation

_____ promotional mix

_____ tariff

_____ cost process

_____ external marketing

_____ monetarism

_____ syndicated loan

_____ estimated market

_____ overtime

_____ controllable cost

_____ win-lose (and win-win) situations

_____ M&A (mergers and acquisitions)

_____ secondary market

Page Total _____

_____ high-powered money

_____ probability distribution

_____ cash flow

_____ convertible preferred stock

_____ equal employment opportunity

_____ product innovation

_____ rediscount

_____ terminal value

_____ commercial banking

_____ network

_____ deductions

_____ countercyclical

_____ transportation cost

_____ management development

_____ maximum expected value

_____ federal funds market

_____ Monte Carlo simulation

_____ cost center

_____ cycle time

_____ private label

_____ Great Depression

_____ intangible asset

_____ F.O.B. shipment

_____ sales lead

_____ accounting systems

_____ queuing theory

_____ end-user computing

Page Total _____

_____ tax avoidance

_____ price elasticity

_____ MBA

_____ capital markets

_____ multiple-period inventory

_____ value chain

_____ regression coefficient

_____ management style

_____ managed float

_____ out-of-pocket cost

_____ product design

_____ operating leverage

_____ dissaving

_____ assets

_____ dependent variable

_____ limit order

_____ pooling method

_____ revenue allowance

_____ PP&E (property, plant, and equipment)

_____ separation of ownership and control

_____ job sequencing

_____ payback period

_____ street name

_____ top-down communication

_____ fixed charge coverage

_____ productivity

_____ controlling interest

Page Total   _____

_____ prime rate

_____ quality circle

_____ accounts payable (and receivable)

_____ constant dollars

_____ investment center

_____ flexible budget

_____ value added

_____ top line

_____ premium

_____ secondary issue

_____ ability-to-pay principle

_____ contingency theory

_____ multiplier effect

_____ fixed position

_____ advertising sales ratio

_____ operating income

_____ field sales force

_____ trading range

_____ price promotion

_____ Marxism

_____ aggregate scheduling

_____ preferred stock

_____ advertising copy

_____ quality of service

_____ gross contribution margin

_____ perfect (and imperfect) information

_____ futures trading

Page Total _____

_____ balanced budget

_____ mass production

_____ tender offer

_____ socialism

_____ mutual goal-setting

_____ Madison Avenue

_____ cash basis of accounting

_____ compound interest

_____ autonomous work group

_____ Chapter 11

_____ annuity

_____ stagflation

_____ media market

_____ Wall Street (the Street)

_____ normal distribution

_____ entrepreneur

_____ sample size

_____ R&D

_____ product usage rate

_____ units-of-output

_____ Taft-Hartley Act

_____ not-for-profit organization

_____ financial structure

_____ direct cost

_____ transfer payment

_____ cost reporting

_____ "what if" questions

Page Total _____

_____ loan loss reserve

_____ Nikkei Index

_____ performance evaluation

_____ EEOC

_____ outplacement

_____ stroking

_____ letter of intent

_____ vertical organization

_____ holding company

_____ GAAP (generally accepted accounting principles)

_____ direct mail

_____ Gramm-Rudman-Hollins Act

_____ Black Monday

_____ retail banking

_____ RFP (request for proposal)

_____ direct salesforce

_____ "me too" product

_____ operations research (or)

_____ purchase method

_____ discretionary account

_____ sampling

_____ underwriter

_____ recession

_____ standard error

_____ incentive compensation

_____ financial analysis

_____ motivation

Page Total _____

_____ zero-sum game

_____ MBWA (management by wandering around)

_____ line of credit

_____ pension plan

_____ cost containment

_____ job design

_____ executive summary

_____ hot stock

_____ contract

_____ front loading

_____ EPS (earnings per share)

_____ Keogh Plan

_____ foreign exchange market intervention

_____ quality of design

_____ lot-for-lot ordering

_____ ISDN (integrated services digital network)

_____ production lot size determination

_____ SBU (strategic business unit)

_____ media scheduling

_____ contingent liabilities

_____ block of stock

_____ standard cost

_____ time value of money

_____ backward integration

_____ FIFO (first in, first out)

_____ bottom line

_____ psychological contract

Page Total _____

_____ sample mean

_____ BCG (growth/share) matrix

_____ petty cash

_____ law of diminishing returns

_____ CAD-CAM

_____ committed cost

_____ NLRB (National Labor Relations Board)

_____ New York Mercantile Exchange

_____ Big Blue

_____ crowding out

_____ MBO (management by objectives)

_____ auditing

_____ marketing strategy

_____ assessed valuation

_____ money stock

_____ Common Market

_____ materials management

_____ capitalization of assets

_____ nominal exchange rate

_____ easy-money policy

_____ deductible

_____ corporate culture

_____ layout by process

_____ task force

_____ Hawthorne effect

_____ least squares regression

_____ Theory X

Page Total _____

_____ capital gains (and losses)

_____ idle capacity

_____ macroeconomics

_____ time-cost tradeoff

_____ breakup value

_____ marginal tax rate

_____ mixed economy

_____ FTC (Federal Trade Commission)

_____ product liability

_____ sales prospect

_____ survey population

_____ sampling error

_____ Pacific Rim

_____ decision support system

_____ headhunter

_____ finished products

_____ distribution channels

_____ automation

_____ cash cow

_____ reorder point

_____ user-friendly

_____ covenant

_____ confidence intervals

_____ fixed asset

_____ documentation

_____ wage incentive plan

_____ National Labor Relations Act

Page Total _____

_____ *Fortune* 500

_____ mature industry

_____ legitimate power

_____ bill of materials

_____ loss leader

_____ manufacturing cost

_____ PR (public relations)

_____ receiving report

_____ capital-intensive

_____ turnaround

_____ referent power

_____ foreign exchange rate

_____ zero coupon bond

_____ perceived value pricing

_____ open economy

_____ sunk cost

_____ collusion

_____ featherbedding

_____ time-motion studies

_____ NPV (net present value)

_____ service operations

_____ product growth

_____ joint venture

_____ capital investment

_____ degrees of freedom

_____ operating cycle

_____ licensing

Page Total _____

_____ social investment

_____ natural rate of unemployment

_____ trade barrier

_____ DP (data processing)

_____ PC

_____ breakeven analysis

_____ social security system

_____ seasonality

_____ programmed cost

_____ discount broker

_____ input controls

_____ round lot

_____ lead time

_____ Laffer curve

_____ COGS (cost of goods sold)

_____ stock market

_____ COMEX

_____ after-tax cash flow

_____ horizontal integration

_____ registered representative

_____ stress management

_____ revenue bond

_____ closed economy

_____ frequency distribution

_____ simulation

_____ bidrigging

_____ black market

Page Total _____

_____ compound value

_____ start-up cost

_____ subsidiary

_____ barriers to entry (and exit)

_____ cost of finished goods

_____ trade union

_____ supply-side economics

_____ network scheduling techniques

_____ annualized revenue

_____ debt restructuring

_____ psychographics

_____ nominal interest rate

_____ production rate

_____ product manager

_____ marginal cost

_____ avoidable cost

_____ merger-related expense

_____ captive market

_____ CFA (chartered financial analyst)

_____ patent

_____ trade bill

_____ finite population

_____ corporate image

_____ unit cost

_____ overhead

_____ general ledger

_____ pure strategies

Page Total _____

_____ return on capital

_____ stockout

_____ insolvency

_____ market broadening

_____ joint costs

_____ non-tariff barrier

_____ profit

_____ subordinated debenture

_____ batch

_____ electronic funds transfer (EFT)

_____ devaluation

_____ money market

_____ expert power

_____ comingled trust

_____ robotics

_____ period cost

_____ subjective probability

_____ IPO (initial public offering)

_____ capital expenditure

_____ deflation

_____ comparable worth

_____ national income

_____ MIS (management information systems)

_____ warrant

_____ nondurable goods

_____ administered prices

_____ purchasing agent

Page Total _____

_____ master production schedule

_____ Edge Act company

_____ extrapolation

_____ public debt

_____ job evaluation

_____ hedging

_____ certification decision

_____ dividend

_____ marketing research

_____ experience curve

_____ economic lot size

_____ SKU (stock keeping unit)

_____ word processing

_____ commodity products

_____ technological leapfrogging

_____ reorganization

_____ production control

_____ conglomerate

_____ methods analysis and improvement

_____ statistical significance

_____ capital structure

_____ span of control

_____ account management

_____ EXIMBANK

_____ variance

_____ process industry

_____ CPU (central processing unit)

Page Total _____

_____ Big Board

_____ kickback

_____ process costing

_____ opinion poll

_____ intrapreneur

_____ economic forecasting

_____ independent-demand inventory

_____ set-up time

_____ real interest rate

_____ standard time

_____ computer graphics

_____ satisficing

_____ Theory Y

_____ turnover

_____ competitive strategy

_____ net income

_____ normal capacity

_____ QWL (quality of working life)

_____ discounting

_____ economies of sale

_____ undifferentiated marketing

_____ interchangeable parts

_____ par value

_____ arrearage

_____ minimum wage

_____ profitability ratios

_____ Eurobond

Page Total _____

_____ bottom-up communication

_____ behavior modification

_____ bar (pie, line, column) chart

_____ bank reserves

_____ complementary products

_____ bonus plan

_____ margins

_____ systematic risk

_____ accounting period

_____ banker's acceptance

_____ MRP (material requirements planning)

_____ hardware

_____ sales mix

_____ New York Stock Exchange (NYSE)

_____ OD (organizational development)

_____ deregulation

_____ line and staff

_____ marginal product

_____ expense budget

_____ effective exchange rate

_____ brand loyalty

_____ LDC (less developed country)

_____ logistic chain

_____ profitability index

_____ double taxation

_____ OPEC (Organization of Petroleum Exporting Countries)

Page Total   _____

_____ watered stock

_____ Delphi method

_____ foreign securities

_____ alienation

_____ placebo effect

_____ revaluation

_____ modem

_____ carriage trade

_____ lease-or-buy decision

_____ flow-line layout

_____ post-merger integration

_____ FASB (Financial Accounting Standards Board)

_____ commercial paper

_____ matrix organization

_____ negotiated bid

_____ pro forma statement

_____ critical path method

_____ short runs

_____ New Deal

_____ price sensitivity

_____ risk arbitrage

_____ point-of-purchase

_____ accelerated depreciation

_____ PAC (political action committee)

_____ M2

_____ interim income statement

_____ financial accounting

Page Total _____

_____ cost allocation

_____ off-balance-sheet financing

_____ unemployment insurance

_____ production cost

_____ communism

_____ independent variable

_____ IT (information technology)

_____ diversification

_____ profit sharing

_____ sales territory

_____ corporate income tax

_____ database management system

_____ game theory

_____ agency bond (or paper)

_____ collective bargaining agreement

_____ central bank

_____ LBO

_____ exempt employee

_____ white knight

_____ redlining

_____ capital recovery factor

_____ partnership

_____ gross profit margin

_____ Group of Seven

_____ umbrella brand

_____ mainframe

Page Total   _____

_____ bimodal distribution

_____ coercive power

_____ capital stock

_____ asset management

_____ risk averse

_____ full employment

_____ common stock

_____ marketing mix

_____ diffusion of innovation

_____ basis point

_____ retained earnings

_____ change agent

_____ delta

_____ predatory pricing

_____ monopoly

_____ standard of living

_____ marketing "myopia"

_____ Europe 1992

_____ tax accounting

_____ collateral

_____ GNP

_____ venture capital

_____ decision theory

_____ fixed cost

_____ proxy fight

_____ capital

Page Total _____

_____ tax shield

_____ SG&A (selling, general, and administrative expenses)

_____ dilution

_____ CEO

_____ durable goods

_____ cumulative distribution

_____ time deposit

_____ price break

_____ massaging the numbers

_____ consolidated financial statement

_____ legal tender

_____ planned obsolescence

_____ oligopoly

_____ cash budget

_____ zero bracket

_____ articles of incorporation

_____ item cost

_____ liquidity ratios

_____ vertical marketing

_____ GDP (gross domestic product)

_____ annual meeting

_____ type II error

_____ OTC (over-the-counter market)

_____ lot sizing

_____ ECU (European Currency Unit)

_____ equity kicker

Page Total _____

_____ formal/informal organization

_____ puts and calls

_____ numerical control

_____ push or pull strategy

_____ participative management

_____ weighted arithmetic mean

_____ correlation coefficient

_____ competitive intelligence

_____ Moody's

_____ leasehold improvements

_____ divestiture

_____ lockout

_____ nonverbal communication

_____ capital goods

_____ balloon payment

_____ policies and procedures

_____ penny stock

_____ delay allowance

_____ dog and pony show

_____ FSLIC (Federal Savings and Loan Insurance Corporation)

_____ market-oriented location

_____ promotional sample

_____ days' sales in inventory

_____ zero-based budgeting

_____ differential cost

_____ standard deviation

Page Total _____

_____ systems architecture

_____ investment portfolio

_____. executive succession

_____ annual report

_____ equilibrium

_____ acceptance sampling

_____ merger

_____ AFL-CIO

_____ inventory turnover

_____ EOQ (economic order quantity)

_____ accounting cycle

_____ property tax

_____ real exchange rate

_____ B-School

_____ low-cost producer

_____ trade promotion

_____ arithmetic mean

_____ unit volume

_____ no-load fund

_____ corporate mission

_____ on-line system

_____ exclusive distribution

_____ focus group

_____ capacity planning

_____ hard disk

_____ OPIC (Overseas Private Investment Corporation)

_____ role ambiguity

Page Total _____

_____ leading indicators

_____ 401(k)

_____ reliability testing

_____ income statement

_____ excise tax

_____ corporate social responsibility

_____ bond rating

_____ shareholder

_____ current market

_____ desktop publishing

_____ product promotion

_____ closely held corporation

_____ organized labor

_____ job sharing

_____ controller

_____ scrap allowance

_____ sole proprietorship

_____ decision-making group

_____ competitiveness

_____ lumpy demand

_____ code of conduct

_____ ROI (return on investment)

_____ capital flow

_____ CBT (Chicago Board of Trade)

_____ tax shelter

_____ activity ratios

_____ trade show

Page Total _____

_____ wage-price controls

_____ trademark

_____ systems integration

_____ board of directors

_____ microeconomics

_____ physical count of inventories

_____ milestone scheduling

_____ bear market

_____ conflict of interest

_____ straddle position

_____ generic brand

_____ takeover target

_____ skim strategy

_____ capital asset pricing model (CAPM)

_____ arbitrage

_____ cold call

_____ efficient market theory

_____ discretionary cost

_____ purchase order

_____ floating exchange rate

_____ shadow price

_____ conspicuous consumption

_____ EPA

_____ test market

_____ sales promotion

_____ fiscal year (FY)

_____ CPI (Consumer Price Index)

Page Total _____

_____ carrying cost

_____ learning curve

_____ accrual basis of accounting

_____ horizontal organizational structure

_____ ROA (return on assets)

_____ advances and declines

_____ industrial relations

_____ sales quota

_____ 10-K

_____ relative prices

_____ Nielsen data

_____ consolidation

_____ contribution

_____ balance of payments

_____ descriptive statistics

_____ SEC (Securities and Exchange Commission)

_____ residual income

_____ group incentive

_____ facility location

_____ utilitarianism

_____ moving average

_____ public interest group

_____ job description

_____ disinvestment

_____ safe harbor

_____ flextime

_____ beta

Page Total _____

_____ golden parachute

_____ decision tree

_____ float

_____ yield to maturity

_____ operations management

_____ escalator clause

_____ labor force

_____ nonmanufacturing operations

_____ Four P's

_____ tax evasion

_____ net contribution

_____ stock purchase plan

_____ executive compensation

_____ return on net worth

_____ inflation

_____ Gantt chart

_____ affirmative action

_____ interest rate

_____ gross income

_____ business ethics

_____ arbitration

_____ PIMS (profit impact of marketing strategy) database

_____ Glass-Steagall Act

_____ COO (chief operating officer)

_____ organization chart

_____ halo effect

Page Total _____

_____ multiple regression

_____ price leader

_____ set-up cost

_____ facility layout

_____ "close to the customer"

_____ input model

_____ export and imports

_____ scab

_____ benefit segmentation

_____ costing

_____ demographics

_____ Dun & Bradstreet

_____ FAX (facsimile)

_____ debenture

_____ seasonal index

_____ OSHA (Occupational Safety and Health Act)

_____ Merc (Chicago Mercantile Exchange)

_____ demand

_____ indexing

_____ dollar cost averaging

_____ effective interest rate

_____ fourth-generation language

_____ marginal propensity to consume (or save)

_____ impulse purchase

_____ junk bond

_____ application software

_____ competition

Page Total _____

_____ market expansion

_____ linear programming

_____ product differentiation

_____ write-off

_____ returns and allowances

_____ IRR (internal rate of return)

_____ gray market

_____ goods in transit

_____ exchange rate

_____ conditional probability

_____ fixed investment

_____ replacement cost

_____ economies of scope

_____ trade credit

_____ overstaffing

_____ ESOP (employee stock ownership plan)

_____ multinational corporation (MNC)

_____ optimization

_____ insider trading

_____ unit time standard

_____ 10-Q

_____ production deadline

_____ shop floor control

_____ yield curve

_____ periodic system

_____ tax credit

_____ defects per unit

Page Total _____

_____ temporary groups

_____ mutual fund

_____ closed-loop feedback

_____ backlog

_____ t-test

_____ Maslow's Hierarchy of Needs

_____ net liability position

_____ high-yield savings

_____ Clayton Antitrust Act

_____ per diem

_____ value analysis

_____ ROE (return on equity)

_____ process life cycle

_____ balance of trade

_____ elasticity of demand

_____ product life cycle (PLC)

_____ capitalism

_____ free trade

_____ total quality management (TQM)

_____ incremental tax rate

_____ niche strategy

_____ buyer's market

_____ decentralized organization

_____ back-order

_____ job-order cost accounting

_____ office automation

_____ treasury stock

Page Total _____

_____ consumption tax

_____ leveraged recapitalization

_____ prudent man rule

_____ Federal Reserve Board

_____ piecework

_____ situational leadership

_____ bull market

_____ personal selling

_____ per capita income

_____ revenue

_____ statement of changes in financial position

_____ internal control

_____ management-by-exception principle

_____ extrinsic reward

_____ perks

_____ market share

_____ return on total assets

_____ SMSA

_____ terms of trade

_____ product portfolio

_____ at the opening (or close)

_____ general systems theory

_____ long-range (and short-range) planning

_____ PPI (producer price index)

_____ sales forecasting

_____ product warranty

_____ embargo

Page Total _____

_____ liquidation

_____ dual career

_____ route sheet

_____ logo

_____ opportunity cost

_____ managerial grid

_____ discount rate

_____ full disclosure

_____ operating system

_____ perceptual map

_____ current dollars

_____ leadership style

_____ reference group

_____ cost systems

_____ Rust Belt

_____ variable cost

_____ financing requirements

_____ penetration strategy

_____ World Bank

_____ tombstone

_____ biased sample

_____ cost accounting

_____ embezzlement

_____ aggregate supply

_____ cost average

_____ ABC analysis

_____ current ratio

Page Total   _____

_____ sales representative

_____ economic feasibility

_____ regulatory agency

_____ fighting brand

_____ personal consumption

_____ NASDAQ (National Association of Securities Dealers Automated Quotation system)

_____ public offering

_____ cost-push inflation

_____ expert system

_____ career planning

_____ general manager

_____ sales force

_____ profit taking

_____ HMO

_____ raw materials

_____ import quota

_____ selection interview

_____ regional marketing

_____ Four Tigers

_____ charter

_____ product screening

_____ stakeholder

_____ aggregate demand

_____ hard copy

_____ product concept

Page Total _____

_____ discount window

_____ quality assurance

_____ minicomputer

_____ minimum cost

_____ make-or-buy decision

_____ spreadsheet program

_____ manual accounting system

_____ CD (certificate of deposit)

_____ sensitivity analysis

_____ finished-goods inventory

_____ audit opinion

_____ random error

_____ producer cooperative

_____ in-process inspection

_____ budget variance

_____ discounts and allowances

_____ corporate climate

_____ planned change

_____ S&P 500

_____ convertible security

_____ stock dividend

_____ controlled-growth strategy

_____ positioning

_____ cash management

_____ silent partner

_____ microcomputer

Page Total _____

_____ strategic planning

_____ portfolio management

_____ yield

_____ risk/return tradeoff

_____ contingency tables

_____ global branding

_____ indirect cost

_____ cost-benefit analysis

_____ demand for money

_____ bank reconciliation

_____ bankruptcy

_____ S&L

_____ production volume

_____ econometrics

_____ logistic management

_____ product quality

_____ corporate raider

_____ hard sell

_____ invoice

_____ brand name

_____ salvage value

_____ forward integration

_____ marginal revenue

_____ materialism

_____ tight money policy

_____ options

_____ blue chip

Page Total _____

_____ red tape

_____ write-down

_____ whistleblower

_____ safety stock

_____ sunset industry

_____ capacity utilization

_____ normative economics

_____ budgeting

_____ market maker

_____ working capital

_____ *perestroika*

_____ skewed distribution

_____ factory system

_____ proxy statement

_____ earnings growth

_____ investment banking

_____ centralized organization

_____ job shop

_____ nepotism

_____ price points

_____ AI (artificial intelligence)

_____ accounts expenses

_____ design for manufacturability

_____ segmentation

_____ M1

_____ market potential

_____ net assets

Page Total _____

_____ line balancing

_____ general journal

_____ missionary sales force

_____ Eurodollar market

Page Total   _____

_____ Checklist Total (sum of page totals)

÷ 1200 Divide checklist total by 1200

= ____

× 100 Multiply by 100

= ____ This figure represents the percentage of the list
with which you are familiar (80% = 960 items).

APPENDIX

THE MANAGERIAL LITERACY LIST: ALPHABETIZED VERSION

This alphabetized list offers a convenient way to cross-check the items on the randomized list. If you want to see whether a particular item appears on the list, this version will obviously help. Remember, however, that an entry may not appear exactly as you have seen or heard it. For instance, you will not find "life cycle" on the list, but you will find "product life cycle (PLC)." You will not find "channels of distribution," but "distribution channels" appears on the list. Similarly, "return on investment" appears as "ROI." Because alphabetizing encourages such single-item checks, and because it dulls some of the natural vigor of the list, we didn't want to provide only an alphabetized version. We are interested in giving managers a chance to assess their familiarity with the whole list (best accomplished with the random version) and then to see where holes in their knowledge appeared.

This list makes it easy to check on those holes. Every entry has been assigned a provenance, a function or field or area with which it is closely associated. Obviously, some entries are associated with more than one area, and in those cases we tried to pick the area that best captured its use or focused its importance. These provenances are marked next to each item with a check under the appropriate category.

There are nine provenances, which may be grouped into three groups of three. The first triad represents the central functions of business: marketing, finance, and operations. The second concerns the analysis, accounting, and reporting of these functions: accounting, statistics, information systems. The third—and bulkiest—triad concerns the overall organizational patterns, policy, and dynamics, as well as the environment in which business functions: economic, legal, and social environment, organizational structure and dynamics, general management perspectives and issues.

	Essential Functions		
	Marketing	Finance	Operations
10-K			
10-Q			
401(k)			
ABC analysis			1
ability-to-pay principle		1	
accelerated depreciation			
acceptance sampling	1		
account management	1		
accounting cycle			
accounting entity concept			
accounting period			
accounting systems			
accounts expenses			
accounts payable (and receivable)			
accrual basis of accounting			
accrued revenue			
achievement motivation			
acquisition			
activity ratios			
administered prices			
advances and declines		1	
advertising copy	1		
advertising/sales ratio	1		
affirmative action			
AFL-CIO			
after-tax cash flow		1	
agency bond (or paper)		1	
aggregate demand			
aggregate scheduling			
aggregate supply			
AI (artificial intelligence)			
alienation			
allocated cost			

Reporting Functions			Organizational Patterns and Policy		
Accounting	Statistics	Information Systems	Economic, Legal, and Social Environment	Organizational Structure and Dynamics	General Management Perspectives and Issues
1					
1					
			1		
1					
1					
1					
1					
1					
1					
1					
1					
1					
				1	
					1
1					
			1		
			1		
			1		
			1		
			1		
			1		
		1			
				1	
1					

	Marketing	Finance	Operations
Essential Functions			
American Stock Exchange (AMEX)		1	
amortization			
annual meeting			
annual report			
annualized revenue			
annuity		1	
antitrust legislation			
application software			
arbitrage		1	
arbitration			
arithmetic mean			
arrearage			
articles of incorporation			
assessed valuation		1	
asset management		1	
assets			
at the opening (or close)		1	
attrition rate			
audit committee			
audit opinion			
auditing			
autocrat			
automation			
autonomous work group			1
avoidable cost			
B-School			
back-order			1
backlog			1
backward integration			1
balance of payments			
balance of trade			
balance sheet			
balanced budget			

| Reporting Functions | | | Organizational Patterns and Policy | | |
Accounting	Statistics	Information Systems	Economic, Legal, and Social Environment	Organizational Structure and Dynamics	General Management Perspectives and Issues
1					
					1
					1
1					
			1		
		1			
			1		
	1				
1					
			1		
1					
				1	
1					
1					
1					
				1	
			1		
1					
			1		
			1		
			1		
1					
			1		

	Essential Functions		
	Marketing	*Finance*	*Operations*
balloon payment		1	
bank reconciliation		1	
bank reserves		1	
banker's acceptance		1	
bankruptcy			
bar (pie, line, column) chart			
bargaining unit			
barriers to entry (and exit)			
base year			
basis point		1	
batch			1
BCG (growth/share) matrix	1		
bear market			
behavior modification			
benefit segmentation	1		
beta		1	
biased sample			
bidrigging			
Big Blue			
Big Board		1	
bill of materials			1
bimodal distribution			
black market			
Black Monday			
blacklisting			
block of stock		1	
blue chip		1	
board of directors			
bond		1	
bond rating		1	
bonus plan			
book value		1	
bottom line			

	Reporting Functions		Organizational Patterns and Policy		
Accounting	Statistics	Information Systems	Economic, Legal, and Social Environment	Organizational Structure and Dynamics	General Management Perspectives and Issues
			1		
				1	
			1		
			1		
			1		
			1		
				1	
	1				
			1		
					1
	1				
			1		
					1
					1
					1
				1	
					1

	Marketing	Finance	Operations
bottom-up communication			
brainstorming session			
brand loyalty	1		
brand management	1		
brand name	1		
breakeven analysis	1		
breakup value			
budget variance			
budgeting			
bull market			
business cycle			
business ethics			
business strategy			
business-as-usual			
buyer's market			
CAD-CAM			1
capacity planning			1
capacity utilization			1
capital		1	
capital asset pricing model (CAPM)		1	
capital budgeting		1	
capital expenditure		1	
capital flow		1	
capital formation		1	
capital gains (and losses)		1	
capital goods		1	
capital investment		1	
capital markets		1	
capital recovery factor			
capital stock		1	
capital structure		1	
capital-intensive		1	
capitalism			

Reporting Functions			Organizational Patterns and Policy		
Accounting	Statistics	Information Systems	Economic, Legal, and Social Environment	Organizational Structure and Dynamics	General Management Perspectives and Issues
				1	
				1	
					1
1					
1					
			1		
			1		
			1		
					1
					1
			1		
1					
			1		

	Essential Functions		
	Marketing	Finance	Operations
capitalization of assets			
captive market			
career planning			
carriage trade	1		
carrying cost			1
cartel			
cash basis of accounting			
cash budget			
cash cow	1		
cash flow		1	
cash management		1	
CBOE (Chicago Board Options Exchange)		1	
CBT (Chicago Board of Trade)		1	
CD (certificate of deposit)		1	
central bank			
centralized organization			
CEO			
certification decision			
CFA (chartered financial analyst)		1	
CFO			
change agent			
Chapter 11			
charter			
classical economics			
Clayton Antitrust Act			
"close to the customer"	1		
closed economy			
closed-loop feedback			
closely held corporation			
code of conduct			
code of ethics			
coercive power			
COGS (cost of goods sold)			

Reporting Functions			Organizational Patterns and Policy		
Accounting	Statistics	Information Systems	Economic, Legal, and Social Environment	Organizational Structure and Dynamics	General Management Perspectives and Issues
1					
			1		
				1	
			1		
	1				
	1				
			1		
					1
					1
			1		
					1
					1
			1		
			1		
			1		
			1		
			1		
				1	
					1
					1
					1
				1	
1					

	Essential Functions		
	Marketing	*Finance*	*Operations*
cold call	1		
collateral		1	
collective bargaining agreement			
collusion			
COMEX		1	
comingled trust		1	
commercial banking			
commercial paper		1	
committed cost			
commodity products	1		
Common Market			
common stock		1	
communism			
comparable worth			
competition			
competitive advantage			
competitive intelligence			
competitive strategy			
competitiveness			
complementary products	1		
compound interest		1	
compound value			1
computer graphics			
conditional probability			
confidence intervals			
conflict management			
conflict of interest			
conglomerate			
consoliated financial statement			
consolidation			
conspicuous consumption			
constant dollars			
consumer benefit	1		

| | Reporting Functions | | Organizational Patterns and Policy | | |
Accounting	Statistics	Information Systems	Economic, Legal, and Social Environment	Organizational Structure and Dynamics	General Management Perspectives and Issues
			1		
					1
			1		
1					
			1		
			1		
1					
			1		
					1
					1
					1
			1		
		1			
	1				
	1				
				1	
					1
			1		
1					
					1
			1		
			1		

	Essential Functions		
	Marketing	*Finance*	*Operations*
consumer protection			
consumerism			
consumption tax			
contingency tables			
contingency theory			
contingent liabilities			
continuous improvement			1
continuous production			1
contracts			
contribution			
controllable cost			
controlled-growth strategy			
controller			
controlling interest			
convertible preferred stock		1	
convertible security		1	
COO (chief operating officer)			
core business			
corporate climate			
corporate culture			
corporate image			
corporate income tax			
corporate mission			
corporate raider			
corporate social responsibility			
corporate strategy			
corrective action			
correlation coefficient			
cost			
cost accounting			
cost allocation			
cost average			
cost behavior			

Reporting Functions			Organizational Patterns and Policy		
Accounting	Statistics	Information Systems	Economic, Legal, and Social Environment	Organizational Structure and Dynamics	General Management Perspectives and Issues
			1		
			1		
			1		
	1				
	1				
1					
			1		
1					
1					
					1
1					
					1
					1
					1
					1
					1
					1
			1		
					1
			1		
					1
					1
				1	
	1				
1					
1					
1					
1					
1					

	Essential Functions		
	Marketing	Finance	Operations
cost center			
cost classification			
cost containment			
cost of capital		1	
cost of finished goods			
cost process			
cost reporting			
cost systems			
cost-benefit analysis			
cost-profit-volume analysis			1
cost-push inflation			
costing			
countercyclical			
couponing	1		
covenant			
CPA			
CPI (Consumer Price Index)			
CPU (central processing unit)			
credit		1	
critical path method			1
crowding out			
CRP (capacity requirements planning)			1
cumulative distribution			
currency appreciation (and depreciation)			
current dollars			
current market			
current ratio		1	
cycle time			1
database			
database management system			
days' sales in accounts receivable			
days' sales in inventory			
debenture		1	

| Reporting Functions | | | Organizational Patterns and Policy | | |
Accounting	Statistics	Information Systems	Economic, Legal, and Social Environment	Organizational Structure and Dynamics	General Management Perspectives and Issues
1					
1					
1					
1					
1					
		1			
		1			
					1
			1		
1					
			1		
			1		
1					
			1		
		1			
			1		
	1				
			1		
			1		
			1		
		1			
		1			
1					
1					

	Marketing	Finance	Operations
debit			
debt		1	
debt restructuring			
debt/equity ratio		1	
decentralized organization			
decision support system			
decision theory			
decision tree			
decision-making group			
deductible			
deductions			
defects per unit			1
deficit spending			
deflation			
degrees of freedom			
delay allowance			1
Delphi method			
delta			
demand			
demand for money			
demographics			
dependent demand			
dependent variable			
depletion allowance			
depreciation			
depression			
deregulation			
derived demand			
descriptive statistics			
design for manufacturability			1
desktop publishing			
devaluation			
differential cost			

| Reporting Functions | | | Organizational Patterns and Policy | | |
Accounting	Statistics	Information Systems	Economic, Legal, and Social Environment	Organizational Structure and Dynamics	General Management Perspectives and Issues
1					
					1
				1	
		1			
	1				
	1				
				1	
1					
1					
			1		
			1		
	1				
					1
	1				
			1		
			1		
			1		
			1		
	1				
			1		
1					
			1		
			1		
			1		
	1				
			1		
			1		
1					

	Essential Functions		
	Marketing	*Finance*	*Operations*
diffusion of innovation			
dilution		1	
direct cost			
direct mail	1		
direct salesforce	1		
discount broker		1	
discount rate			
discount window			
discounted cash flow		1	
discounting	1		
discounts and allowances			
discretionary account			
discretionary cost			
disequilibrium			
disinflation			
disinvestment			
disposable income			
dissaving			
distributed data processing			
distribution channels	1		
diversification			
divestiture			
dividend		1	
division of labor			1
divisional structure			
documentation			
dog and pony show			
dollar cost averaging			
double taxation			
Dow Jones Industrial Average (the Dow)			
downsizing			
DP (data processing)			
dual career			

Reporting Functions			Organizational Patterns and Policy		
Accounting	Statistics	Information Systems	Economic, Legal, and Social Environment	Organizational Structure and Dynamics	General Management Perspectives and Issues
			1		
1					
			1		
			1		
1					
1					
1					
			1		
			1		
			1		
			1		
			1		
		1			
					1
					1
					1
		1			
				1	
1					
			1		
			1		
					1
		1			
				1	

	Essential Functions		
	Marketing	Finance	Operations
Dun & Bradstreet		1	
durable goods			
earnings growth		1	
easy-money policy			
EBIT (earnings before income tax)			
econometrics			
economic feasibility			
economic forecasting			
economic lot size			1
economies of scale			
economies of scope			
ECU (European Currency Unit)			
Edge Act company			
EEC (European Economic Community)			
EEOC			
effective exchange rate			
effective interest rate			
efficient market theory			
elasticity of demand			
electronic funds transfer (EFT)		1	
electronic mail (E-mail)			
embargo			
embezzlement			
end-user computing			
entrepreneur			
EOQ (economic order quantity)			1
EPA			
EPS (earnings per share)		1	
equal employment opportunity			
equilibrium			
equity			
equity capital		1	
equity kicker		1	

	Reporting Functions		Organizational Patterns and Policy		
Accounting	Statistics	Information Systems	Economic, Legal, and Social Environment	Organizational Structure and Dynamics	General Management Perspectives and Issues
			1		
			1		
1					
			1		
			1		
			1		
					1
					1
			1		
			1		
			1		
			1		
			1		
			1		
			1		
			1		
		1			
			1		
					1
		1			
				1	
			1		
			1		
			1		
1					

	Marketing	Finance	Operations
escalator clause		1	
ESOP (employee stock ownership plan)			
estimated market	1		
Eurobond		1	
Eurodollar market		1	
Europe 1992			
exchange rate		1	
excise tax			
exclusive distribution	1		
executive compensation			
executive succession			
executive summary			
exempt employee			
EXIMBANK			
expense budget			
experience curve			1
expert power			
expert system			
exponential smoothing			
exports and imports			
external marketing	1		
extrapolation			
extrinsic reward			
F.O.B. shipment			1
facility layout			1
facility location			1
factory system			1
FASB (Financial Accounting Standards Board)			
FAX (facsimile)			
FDIC			
featherbedding			
Fed wire		1	
federal funds market			

Essential Functions

Reporting Functions			Organizational Patterns and Policy		
Accounting	Statistics	Information Systems	Economic, Legal, and Social Environment	Organizational Structure and Dynamics	General Management Perspectives and Issues
			1		
			1		
			1		
					1
					1
				1	
				1	
			1		
1					
				1	
		1			
	1				
			1		
	1				
				1	
	1				
		1			
			1		
			1		
			1		

	Essential Functions		
	Marketing	*Finance*	*Operations*
Federal Reserve Board			
FICA			
field sales force	1		
FIFO (first in, first out)			1
fighting brand	1		
financial accounting			
financial analysis		1	
financial structure		1	
financing requirements		1	
finished-goods inventory			1
finished products			1
finite population			
fiscal policy			
fiscal year (FY)			
fixed asset			
fixed charge coverage			
fixed cost			
fixed exchange rate			
fixed investment			
fixed manufacturing overhead			
fixed position		1	
flat organization			
flextime			
flexible budget			
float		1	
floating capacity		1	
floating exchange rate			
flow chart			1
flow-line layout			1
focus group	1		
foreign exchange market intervention			
foreign exchange rate			
foreign securities		1	

Reporting Functions			Organizational Patterns and Policy		
Accounting	Statistics	Information Systems	Economic, Legal, and Social Environment	Organizational Structure and Dynamics	General Management Perspectives and Issues
			1		
			1		
1					
	1				
			1		
1					
1					
1					
1					
			1		
			1		
1					
				1	
				1	
1					
			1		
			1		
			1		

	Essential Functions		
	Marketing	*Finance*	*Operations*
formal/informal organization			
Fortress Europe			
Fortune 500			
forward integration			
Four P's	1		
Four Tigers			
fourth-generation language			
franchise	1		
free trade			
frequency distribution			
front loading		1	
FSLIC (Federal Savings & Loan Insurance Corporation)			
FTC (Federal Trade Commission)			
full disclosure			
full employment			
futures trading		1	
GAAP (Generally Accepted Accounting Principles)			
game theory			
Gantt chart			
GATT (General Agreement on Tariffs & Trade)			
GDP (gross domestic product)			
general journal			
general ledger			
general manager			
general systems theory			
generic brand	1		
Glass-Steagall Act			
global branding	1		
global market			
GNP			
gold standard			

Reporting Functions			Organizational Patterns and Policy		
Accounting	Statistics	Information Services	Economic, Legal, and Social Environment	Organizational Structure and Dynamics	General Management Perspectives and Issues
				1	
			1		
			1		
					1
			1		
		1			
			1		
	1				
			1		
			1		
					1
			1		
1					
	1				
					1
			1		
			1		
1					
1					
					1
		1			
			1		
					1
			1		
			1		

	Essential Functions		
	Marketing	*Finance*	*Operations*
golden handcuffs			
golden parachute			
goods in transit			1
goodwill			
Gramm-Rudman-Hollins Act			
gray market			
Great Depression			
greenmail			
Gresham's Law			
gross contribution margin		1	
gross income			
gross profit margin		1	
group incentive			
Group of Seven			
group process			
halo effect			
hands-on manager			
hard copy			
hard disk			
hard sell	1		
hardware			
Hawthorne effect			
headhunter			
hedging		1	
high-powered money		1	
high-yield savings		1	
historical cost			
HMO			
holding company			
horizontal integration			
horizontal organization structure			
hostile takeover			
hot stock		1	

| Reporting Functions | | | Organizational Patterns and Policy | | |
Accounting	Statistics	Information Systems	Economic, Legal, and Social Environment	Organizational Structure and Dynamics	General Management Perspectives and Issues
				1	
				1	
1					
			.1		
					1
			1		
					1
					1
1					
				1	
			1		
				1	
				1	
				1	
		1			
		1			
		1			
				1	
				1	
1					
			1		
			1		
					1
				1	
					1

	Essential Functions		
	Marketing	*Finance*	*Operations*
HRM (human resource management)			
hurdle rate		1	
hyperinflation			
idle capacity			1
IMF (International Monetary Fund)			
import quota			
impulse purchase	1		
in-process inspection			1
incentive compensation			
income statement			
incremental cost			
incremental tax rate			
independent variable			
independent-demand inventory			1
indexing			
indirect cost			
industrial policy			
industrial relations			
inflation			
input controls			1
input model			1
insider trading			
insolvency		1	
intangible asset			
intensive distribution	1		
interchangeable parts			1
interest rate		1	
intergroup conflict			
interim income statement			
interlocking directorates			
internal control			
internal marketing	1		
intrapreneur			

	Reporting Functions		Organizational Patterns and Policy		
Accounting	Statistics	Information Services	Economic, Legal, and Social Environment	Organizational Structure and Dynamics	General Management Perspectives and Issues
				1	
			1		
			1		
			1		
				1	
1					
1					
1					
	1				
			1		
1					
			1		
				1	
			1		
					1
1					
				1	
1					
			1		
1					
					1

	Essential Functions		
	Marketing	Finance	Operations
intrinsic reward			
inventory			1
inventory turnover			1
investment banking		1	
investment center		1	
investment portfolio		1	
investment tax credit			
Invisible Hand			
invoice			1
IPO (initial public offering)		1	
IRR (internal rate of return)		1	
IRS (Internal Revenue Service)			
ISDN (integrated services digital network)			
IT (information technology)			
item cost			
J-I-T (just-in-time)			1
job description			
job design			
job enrichment			
job evaluation			1
job rotation			
job satisfaction			
job security			
job sequencing			1
job sharing			
job shop			1
job-order cost accounting			
jobber			1
joint costs			
joint venture			
judgmental forecasting			
junk bond		1	
Keogh Plan			

Reporting Functions			Organizational Patterns and Policy		
Accounting	Statistics	Information Systems	Economic, Legal, and Social Environment	Organizational Structure and Dynamics	General Management Perspectives and Issues
				1	
1					
			1		
1					
		1			
		1			
1					
				1	
				1	
				1	
				1	
				1	
			1		
				1	
1					
1					
				1	
	1				
			1		

	Essential Functions		
	Marketing	*Finance*	*Operations*
kickback			
labor force			
Laffer curve			
laissez-faire			
LAN (local area network)			
latent market	1		
law of diminishing returns			
law of supply and demand			
layout by process			1
LBO		1	
LDC (less developed country)			
lead time			1
leadership style			
leading indicators			
learning curve			1
lease-or-buy decision		1	
leasehold improvements			
least squares regression			
ledger account			
legal tender			
legitimate power			
letter of credit		1	
letter of intent			
leverage ratios		1	
leveraged recapitalization		1	
liabilities			
licensing		1	
LIFO (last-in, first-out)			1
limit order		1	
line and staff			
line balancing			1
line of credit		1	
linear programming			

Reporting Functions			Organizational Patterns and Policy		
Accounting	Statistics	Information Systems	Economic, Legal, and Social Environment	Organizational Structure and Dynamics	General Management Perspectives and Issues
					1
			1		
			1		
			1		
		1			
			1		
			1		
			1		
				1	
			1		
1					
	1				
1					
			1		
				1	
			1		
1					
				1	
	1				

	Essential Functions		
	Marketing	Finance	Operations
linear regression			
liquidation		1	
liquidity ratios		1	
listed stock		1	
loading		1	
loan loss reserve		1	
lockout			
logistic chain			1
logistic management			1
logo	1		
long-range (and short-range) planning			
loss leader	1		
lot sizing			1
lot-for-lot ordering			1
low-cost producer			
lumpy demand	1		
M&A (mergers and acquisitions)		1	
M1			
M2			
Ma Bell			
macroeconomics			
Madison Avenue	1		
mainframe			
make-or-buy decision		1	
managed float		1	
management audit			
management development			
management style			
management team			
management-by-exception principle			
managerial grid			
manual accounting system			
manufacturer's rep	1		

	Reporting Functions		Organizational Patterns and Policy		
Accounting	Statistics	Information Systems	Economic, Legal, and Social Environment	Organizational Structure and Dynamics	General Management Perspectives and Issues
	1				
			1		
					1
					1
			1		
			1		
			1		
			1		
		1			
					1
				1	
					1
					1
					1
					1
1					

	Essential Functions		
	Marketing	Finance	Operations
manufacturing cost			1
marginal analysis	1		
marginal cost	1		
marginal product	1		
marginal propensity to consume (or save)			
marginal revenue	1		
marginal tax rate			
margins	1		
market broadening	1		
market demand	1		
market expansion	1		
market followers	1		
market growth rate	1		
market maker		1	
market order		1	
market penetration	1		
market potential	1		
market share	1		
market-oriented location	1		
marketing "myopia"	1		
marketing mix	1		
marketing research	1		
marketing strategy	1		
markup	1		
Marxism			
Maslow's Hierarchy of Needs			
mass market	1		
mass production			1
massaging the numbers			
master production schedule			1
materialism			
materials management			1
matrix organization			

Reporting Functions			Organizational Patterns and Policy		
Accounting	Statistics	Information Systems	Economic, Legal, and Social Environment	Organizational Structure and Dynamics	General Management Perspectives and Issues
			1		
			1		
			1		
				1	
					1
			1		
				1	

	Marketing	Finance	Operations
mature industry			
maximum expected value			
MBA			
MBO (management by objectives)			
MBWA (management by wandering around)			
mean time between failures			1
media market	1		
media scheduling	1		
median			
Merc (Chicago Mercantile Exchange)			
merchandising	1		
merger			
merger-related expense			
methods analysis and improvement			1
"me too" product	1		
microcomputer			
microeconomics			
middle management			
milestone scheduling			1
minicomputer			
minimum cost		1	
minimum rate of return		1	
minimum wage			
MIS (management information systems)			
missionary sales force	1		
MITI			
mixed economy			
MLP (master limited partnership)			
mode			
modem			
monetarism			
monetary base			
monetary indicator			

Essential Functions

| Reporting Functions | | | Organizational Patterns and Policy | | |
Accounting	Statistics	Information Systems	Economic, Legal, and Social Environment	Organizational Structure and Dynamics	General Management Perspectives and Issues
			1		
	1				
			1		
					1
					1
	1				
			1		
					1
1					
		1			
			1		
				1	
		1			
			1		
		1			
			1		
			1		
			1		
	1				
		1			
			1		
			1		
			1		

	Essential Functions		
	Marketing	Finance	Operations
monetary policy			
money center bank			
money manager		1	
money market		1	
money stock		1	
money supply			
monopoly			
Monte Carlo simulation			
Moody's		1	
motivation			
moving average			
MRP (material requirements planning)			1
multinational corporation (MNC)			
multiple regression			
multiple-period inventory			1
multiplier effect			
mutual fund		1	
mutual goal-setting			
NASDAQ (National Association of Securities Dealers Automated Quotation System)		1	
national debt			
national income			
National Labor Relations Act			
natural monopoly			
natural rate of unemployment			
negotiated bid		1	
nepotism			
net assets			
net contribution			
net income		1	
net liability position			
net worth		1	
network			

Reporting Functions			Organizational Patterns and Policy		
Accounting	Statistics	Information Systems	Economic, Legal, and Social Environment	Organizational Structure and Dynamics	General Management Perspectives and Issues
			1		
			1		
			1		
			1		
	1				
				1	
	1				
					1
	1				
			1		
				1	
			1		
			1		
			1		
			1		
			1		
					1
1					
1					
1					
				1	

	Essential Functions		
	Marketing	Finance	Operations
network scheduling techniques	1		
New Deal			
New York Mercantile Exchange		1	
New York Stock Exchange (NYSE)		1	
niche strategy	1		
Nielsen data	1		
Nikkei Index		1	
NLRB (National Labor Relations Board)			
no-load fund		1	
nominal exchange rate			
nominal GNP			
nominal interest rate			
non-tariff barrier			
nondurable goods			
nonmanufacturing operations			1
nonverbal communication			
normal capacity			1
normal distribution			
normative economics			
not-for-profit organization			
notes payable (and receivable)			
NPV (net present value)		1	
numerical control			1
objective function			
OD (organizational development)			
off-balance-sheet financing		1	
office automation			
oligopoly			
on-line system			
OPEC (Organization of Petroleum Exporting Countries)			
open economy			
operating cycle			1

	Reporting Functions		Organizational Patterns and Policy		
Accounting	Statistics	Information Systems	Economic, Legal, and Social Environment	Organizational Structure and Dynamics	General Management Perspectives and Issues
			1		
			1		
			1		
			1		
			1		
			1		
			1		
				1	
	1				
			1		
					1
1					
	1				
				1	
		1			
			1		
		1			
			1		
			1		

	Marketing	Finance	Operations
Essential Functions			
operating income			
operating leverage		1	
operating system			
operational budgeting			
operations management			1
operations research (OR)			1
OPIC (Overseas Private Investment Corporation)			
opinion polls			
opportunity cost			
optimization			
optional feature pricing	1		
options		1	
organization chart			
organizational structure			
organized labor			
OSHA (Occupational Safety and Health Act)			
OTC (over-the-counter market)		1	
out-of-pocket cost			
outplacement			
overhead			
overstaffing			
overtime			
owners' equity			
P&L (profit and loss)		1	
P/E ratio		1	
PAC (political action committee)			
Pacific Rim			
par value		1	
partial sampling			
participative management			
partnership			
patent			
payback period		1	

Reporting Functions			Organizational Patterns and Policy		
Accounting	Statistics	Information Systems	Economic, Legal, and Social Environment	Organizational Structure and Dynamics	General Management Perspectives and Issues
1					
		1			
1					
			1		
			1		
					1
	1				
				1	
				1	
			1		
			1		
1					
				1	
1					
				1	
				1	
1					
			1		
			1		
	1				
					1
			1		
			1		

	Marketing	Finance	Operations
payroll			
PC			
penetration strategy	1		
penny stock		1	
pension plan			
per capita income			
per diem			
perceived value pricing	1		
perceptual map	1		
perestroika			
perfect (and imperfect) competition			
perfect (and imperfect) information			
performance evaluation			
period cost			
periodic system			1
perks			
personal consumption			
personal selling	1		
PERT (program evaluation and review technique)			
Peter Principle			
petty cash			
Phillips curve			
physical count of inventories			1
piecework			1
PIMS (profit impact of marketing strategy) database			
placebo effect			
planned change			
planned obsolescence			
point-of-purchase	1		
poison pill			
policies and procedures			

Reporting Functions			Organizational Patterns and Policy		
Accounting	Statistics	Information Systems	Economic, Legal, and Social Environment	Organizational Structure and Dynamics	General Management Perspectives and Issues
1					
		1			
1					
			1		
1					
			1		
					1
					1
				1	
1					
				1	
			1		
					1
					1
1					
			1		
					1
				1	
					1
					1
					1
					1

	Essential Functions		
	Marketing	*Finance*	*Operations*
pooling method			
portfolio management		1	
position power			
positioning	1		
post-merger integration			
postpurchase behavior	1		
potential GNP			
PP&E (property, plant, and equipment)			
PPI (producer price index)			
PR (public relations)			
practical capacity			1
precontract planning			1
predatory pricing			
preferred stock		1	
premium	1		
present value		1	
price break	1		
price cuts	1		
price elasticity			
price leader	1		
price points	1		
price promotion	1		
price sensitivity	1		
prime rate			
prisoner's dilemma			
private label	1		
private placement		1	
pro forma statement		1	
probability distribution			
process costing			
process industry			
process life cycle			1
producer cooperative			

Reporting Functions			Organizational Patterns and Policy		
Accounting	Statistics	Information Systems	Economic, Legal, and Social Environment	Organizational Structure and Dynamics	General Management Perspectives and Issues
	1				
				1	
					1
			1		
1					
			1		
					1
			1		
			1		
			1		
	1				
	1				
1					
			1		
			1		

	Essential Functions		
	Marketing	Finance	Operations
product concept	1		
product design	1		
product differentiation	1		
product growth	1		
product innovation	1		
product liability			
product life cycle (PLC)	1		
product line	1		
product manager	1		
product portfolio	1		
product promotion	1		
product quality			1
product screening	1		
product substitution	1		
product usage rate	1		
product warranty	1		
production control			1
production cost			1
production deadline			1
production lot size determination			1
production rate			1
production volume			1
productivity			
profit			
profit center			
profit sharing			
profit taking		1	
profitability index		1	
profitability ratios		1	
program trading		1	
programmed cost			
programming language			
projected cost			

Reporting Functions			Organizational Patterns and Policy		
Accounting	Statistics	Information Systems	Economic, Legal, and Social Environment	Organizational Structure and Dynamics	General Management Perspectives and Issues
			1		
					1
1					
					1
					1
1					
		1			
1					

	Marketing	Finance	Operations
promissory note		1	
promotional mix	1		
promotional pricing	1		
promotional sample	1		
property tax			
prospectus		1	
protectionism			
proxy fight			
proxy statement			
prudent man rule			
psychographics	1		
psychological contract			
public debt			
public interest group			
public offering		1	
purchase method			1
purchase order			1
purchasing agent			1
purchasing power			
pure strategies			
push or pull strategy	1		
puts and calls		1	
quality assurance			1
quality circle			
quality of design			1
quality of service			1
quantity discount			1
queuing theory			1
QWL (quality of working life)			
R&D			
random error			
random number			
raw materials			1

Essential Functions

| Reporting Functions | | | Organizational Patterns and Policy | | |
Accounting	Statistics	Information Systems	Economic, Legal, and Social Environment	Organizational Structure and Dynamics	General Management Perspectives and Issues
1					
			1		
					1
			1		
			1		
				1	
			1		
			1		
			1		
					1
				1	
				1	
				1	
	1				
	1				

	Essential Functions		
	Marketing	*Finance*	*Operations*
Reaganomics			
real exchange rate			
real GNP			
real interest rate			
receiving report			1
recession			
red tape			
rediscount		1	
redlining			
reference group			
referent power			
regional marketing	1		
registered representative		1	
regression analysis			
regression coefficient			
regressive tax			
regulatory agency			
relative prices	1		
relevant inventory cost			
reliability testing			1
reorder point			1
reorganization			
replacement cost			
repo (repurchase agreement)		1	
residual income			
residual value			
resource allocation			
responsibility accounting			
restructuring			
retail banking			
retained earnings			
return on capital		1	
return on incremental investment		1	

Reporting Functions			Organizational Patterns and Policy		
Accounting	Statistics	Information Systems	Economic, Legal, and Social Environment	Organizational Structure and Dynamics	General Management Perspectives and Issues
			1		
			1		
			1		
			1		
			1		
					1
			1		
				1	
				1	
	1				
	1				
			1		
			1		
1					
					1
1					
1					
1					
					1
1					
					1
			1		
1					

	Essential Functions		
	Marketing	Finance	Operations
return on net worth		1	
return on total assets		1	
returns and allowances	1		
revaluation		1	
revenue			
revenue allowance		1	
revenue bond		1	
RFP (request for proposal)			
risk arbitrage		1	
risk averse			
risk/return tradeoff		1	
ROA (return on assets)		1	
Robinson-Patman Act of 1936			
robotics			
ROE (return on equity)		1	
ROI (return on investment)		1	
role ambiguity			
role conflict			
round lot		1	
route sheet			1
Rust Belt			
S&L			
S&P 500		1	
safe harbor		1	
safety stock		1	
sales force	1		
sales forecasting	1		
sales lead	1		
sales mix	1		
sales promotion	1		
sales prospect	1		
sales quota	1		
sales representative	1		

Reporting Functions			Organizational Patterns and Policy		
Accounting	Statistics	Information Systems	Economic, Legal, and Social Environment	Organizational Structure and Dynamics	General Management Perspectives and Issues
1					
		1			
				1	
			1		
			1		
				1	
				1	
			1		
			1		

Essential Functions

	Marketing	Finance	Operations
sales territory	1		
salvage value			
sample mean			
sample size			
sampling			
sampling error			
satisficing			
savings			
SBU (strategic business unit)			
scab			
scrap allowance			1
sealed bid pricing			
seasonal index			
seasonality			
SEC (Securities and Exchange Commission)			
secondary issue		1	
secondary market		1	
segmentation	1		
selection interview			
selective perception			
self-actualization			
sensitivity analysis			
separable cost			
separation of ownership and control			
sequential sampling			
serial bonds		1	
service economy			
service operations			1
set-up cost			1
set-up time			1
SG&A (selling, general, and administrative expenses			
shadow price			

	Reporting Functions		Organizational Patterns and Policy		
Accounting	Statistics	Information Systems	Economic, Legal, and Social Environment	Organizational Structure and Dynamics	General Management Perspectives and Issues
1					
	1				
	1				
	1				
	1				
			1		
			1		
					1
					1
			1		
			1		
			1		
			1		
				1	
				1	
				1	
	1				
1					
			1		
	1				
			1		
1					
			1		

	Marketing	Finance	Operations
		Essential Functions	
shareholder			
shark repellent			1
Sherman Antitrust Act			
shop floor control			1
short runs			1
silent partner			
simulation			
single proprietorship			
situational leadership			
skewed distribution			
skim pricing	1		
skim strategy	1		
SKU (stock keeping unit)	1		
slush fund			
SMSA	1		
social investment			
social security system			
socialism			
sole proprietorship			
span of control			
specialization of labor			
specialty goods	1		
spinoff			
spreadsheet program			
stagflation			
stakeholder			
standard cost			
standard data			
standard deviation			
standard error			
standard of living			
standard time			1
start date			1

Reporting Functions			Organizational Patterns and Policy		
Accounting	Statistics	Information Systems	Economic, Legal, and Social Environment	Organizational Structure and Dynamics	General Management Perspectives and Issues
			1		
			1		
			1		
	1				
			1		
				1	
	1				
1					
					1
			1		
			1		
			1		
					1
			1		
					1
		1			
			1		
					1
1					
	1				
	1				
	1				
			1		

	Essential Functions		
	Marketing	Finance	Operations
start-up cost		1	
state unemployment compensation tax			
statement of changes in financial position			
statistical signifiance			
stock average		1	
stock dividend		1	
stock market		1	
stock option		1	
stock purchase plan		1	
stock split		1	
stockout			1
stockout cost			1
straddle position		1	
straight-line depreciation			
strategic planning			
street name		1	
stress management			
strike price		1	
stroking			
strong dollar			
structural unemployment			
Subchapter S corporation			
subcontracting			1
subjective probability			
subordinated debenture		1	
subsidiary			
subsidy			
sunk cost			
sunset industry			
sunset provision			
supply-side economics			
survey population			
sustainable growth			

| Reporting Functions | | | Organizational Patterns and Policy | | |
Accounting	Statistics	Information Systems	Economic, Legal, and Social Environment	Organizational Structure and Dynamics	General Management Perspectives and Issues
			1		
1					
	1				
1					
					1
				1	
				1	
			1		
			1		
			1		
	1				
			1		
			1		
					1
			1		
					1
			1		
	1				
					1

	Marketing	Finance	Operations
Essential Functions			

	Marketing	Finance	Operations
swap		1	
syndicated loan		1	
syndication		1	
systematic risk		1	
systems architecture			
systems integration			
T-bill (treasury bill)			
t-test			
Taft-Hartley Act			
takeover target			
target market	1		
tariff			
task force			
tax accounting			
tax avoidance			
tax credit			
tax evasion			
tax shelter		1	
tax shield			
team building			
technological leapfrogging			
telemarketing	1		
temporary groups			
tender offer		1	
terminal value			
termination			
terms of trade			
test market	1		
the Fed (Federal Reserve System)			
Theory X			
Theory Y			
Theory Z			
tie-in promotion	1		

Reporting Functions			Organizational Patterns and Policy		
Accounting	Statistics	Information Systems	Economic, Legal, and Social Environment	Organizational Structure and Dynamics	General Management Perspectives and Issues
		1			
		1			
			1		
	1				
			1		
					1
			1		
				1	
1					
					1
1					
			1		
1					
				1	
			1		
				1	
1					
				1	
			1		
			1		
				1	
				1	
				1	

	Essential Functions		
	Marketing	*Finance*	*Operations*
tight money policy			
time deposit		1	
time value of money		1	
time-cost tradeoff			1
time-motion studies			1
time-series analysis			1
tombstone		1	
top line			
top management			
top-down communication			
total quality management (TQM)			1
trade barrier			
trade bill			
trade credit			
trade discount	1		
trade promotion	1		
trade show	1		
trade surplus (or deficit)			
trademark			
trade union			
trading range		1	
transfer payment			
transfer pricing			
transportation cost			1
treasury stock			
trial balance			
turnaround			
turnover			1
type A			
type I error			
type II error			
UAW			
umbrella brand	1		

	Reporting Functions		Organizational Patterns and Policy		
Accounting	Statistics	Information Systems	Economic, Legal, and Social Environment	Organizational Structure and Dynamics	General Management Perspectives and Issues
			1		
1					
				1	
				1	
			1		
			1		
			1		
			1		
			1		
			1		
			1		
			1		
			1		
1					
					1
				1	
	1				
	1				
			1		

	Essential Functions		
	Marketing	Finance	Operations
uncollectible account			
underground economy			
underwriter		1	
undifferentiated marketing	1		
unemployment insurance			
unit cost			1
unit time standard			1
unit volume			1
units-of-output			1
user-friendly			
utilitarianism			
value added			
value analysis			
value chain			1
variable cost			
variance			
VAT (value added tax)			
velocity of money			
venture capital		1	
vertical integration			
vertical marketing	1		
vertical organization			
voice mail			
wage incentive plan			
wage-price controls			
Wall Street (the Street)			
warrant		1	
watered stock		1	
weighted arithmetic mean			
weighted average cost of capital		1	
"what-if" questions			
whistleblower			
white knight			

Reporting Functions			Organizational Patterns and Policy		
Accounting	Statistics	Information Systems	Economic, Legal, and Social Environment	Organizational Structure and Dynamics	General Management Perspectives and Issues
1					
			1		
			1		
		1			
					1
					1
					1
1					
	1				
			1		
			1		
					1
				1	
		1			
			1		
			1		
			1		
	1				
					1
					1
					1

	Essential Functions		
	Marketing	_Finance_	_Operations_
win-lose (and win-win) situations			
withholding tax			
word processing			
workstation			
work-in-process inventory			1
working capital	1		
World Bank			
write-down			
write-off			
yield		1	
yield curve		1	
yield rate on bonds		1	
yield to maturity		1	
zero bracket			
zero coupon bond		1	
zero defects			1
zero-based budgeting			
zero-sum game			
	131	203	125

Reporting Functions			Organizational Patterns and Policy		
Accounting	Statistics	Information Systems	Economic, Legal, and Social Environment	Organizational Structure and Dynamics	General Management Perspectives and Issues
				1	
			1		
		1			
		1			
			1		
1					
1					
1					
					1
				1	
141	65	45	284	103	109

ABOUT THE AUTHORS . . .

Gary Shaw is a member of the faculty of the School of Business Administration at the College of William and Mary. He was formerly an Assistant Professor at the Colgate Darden Graduate School of Business Administration at the University of Virginia, where he headed the communication program.

Shaw was educated at the State University of New York at Buffalo and the University of Virginia, where he received his doctorate. Dr. Shaw conducts workshops and consults extensively with managers and executives on effective communication, conflict management, managerial literacy, and ethics. He is co-director of The Foundation for Managerial Literacy located in Williamsburg, Virginia.

Jack Weber is a member of the faculty of the Darden Graduate School of Business Administration at the University of Virginia. His academic credits include posts at the Amos Tuck School of Business Administration at Dartmouth College and the International Management Development Institute in Lausanne, Switzerland, where he served as Visiting Professor of Business Administration and authored a book on European general managers. Prior to his academic career, Professor Weber was with the IBM Corporation.

Weber was educated at Yale, Miami, and the University of California where he received his Ph.D degree in Business Administration and Organizational Behavior. Dr. Weber consults and lectures widely to senior executives and managers in the areas of strategic leadership, managerial literacy, and organizational change. He is also co-director of The Foundation for Managerial Literacy and a principal of The Cahill-Weber Group, a management consulting firm in Charlottesville, Virginia.